Gratefully: warmly or deeply appreciated
of kindness or benefits received.

This book is gratefully dedicated to my
family, friends & freedom of choice.

1st GENERATION *Rich*

Mark J. Migliaccio

ARCHWAY PUBLISHING

Archway Publishing books may be ordered through booksellers or by contacting:

Archway Publishing
1663 Liberty Drive
Bloomington, IN 47403
www.archwaypublishing.com
1 (888) 242-5904

Thanks to Wendy Spalsbury with **One**Creative.

ISBN: 978-1-4808-9204-0 (sc)
ISBN: 978-1-4808-9205-7 (hc)
ISBN: 978-1-4808-9203-3 (e)

Library of Congress Control Number: 2020914346

Print information available on the last page.

Archway Publishing rev. date: 08/24/2020

CONTENTS

"It's doing something that excites you that makes Mondays feel more like Fridays."

PREFACE

MAKING MONDAYS FEEL JUST LIKE FRIDAYS

Are you lost, in a rut, bored, searching, curious, or just undecided about what you were put on earth to do or what career path you should take? Take a second to think about it. Am I wasting away at a dead-end job with no real options? Can I see myself working here till I retire or for the next several years?

My mission in writing this book was to open the eyes of anyone who always wanted to start a business or invest in real estate but never knew how to get started. I want to show that there are many more options to the daily grind and working in a job you dislike with people you would never invite to one of your barbecues.

There must be more to life than just punching a clock and working the same old job until you might get the chance to retire in twenty-five years.

Why is this the norm? Millions and millions of people are stuck working in lifeless environments and doing jobs they can't tolerate. Everyone seems to always be complaining about their jobs but they don't do anything about it.

WHY DO SO MANY PEOPLE JUST SETTLE INTO SOMETHING THEY END UP HATING?

Is there a way to be satisfied—even joyful—or to feel a sense of accomplishment when working? Or is this just some out-of-touch fantasy people have.

I found a group of people who are constantly excited about working. Every day feels like Friday to this group. They have a completely different way of viewing their work. They find their work extremely satisfying. They get excited about—and even look forward to—Mondays. They have goals, vision, and a unique outlook when it comes to their work. They want to change people's lives, and they want to change the entire world. They found out what makes them unique and turned it into something great, which everyone can benefit from.

This group of people never answers to just one boss; they answer to hundreds or even thousands of different bosses. These bosses are called customers. They know if the customer is happy, they get paid—and they get paid well.

I tackle these topics by building a case that anyone can have a great chance of being successful when it comes to starting their own business. What does it really take to find a niche and build something that will give you the cash you need to invest in other areas, including real estate?

I have not met a person yet who has not had a dream of being their own boss, running their own company, buying or flipping real estate, developing and then selling something to the whole world, and building a large cash machine that pays all their expenses every month.

That's exactly what we did, and I share in detail how we did it.

POV

Some people have an unhealthy perspective when it comes to how they view their money. I want to bring a different point of view on this topic. People should see money as a valuable tool and not taboo. Money being used to help instead of hinder.

This book is **not** about the love of money but the function of it. Multiple generations never learned the real **freedom** that money can provide. Knowledge dies if it's never put into practice.

People in general don't like to talk about money. That's where the problem starts. Every soul on earth uses this great tool every day without a though. That would be the 2nd problem. Money needs a master and someone willing to take the time to master it. Money will patiently wait for its owners' thoughtful directions.

When you really care about something you're going to pay attention to it. Your hard-earned money needs your full attention and guidance. Money is waiting for a wise, long-sighted leader for its orders. A great relationship is built on effort, patience and tine. Build a lasting bond with your money that will take you into a comfortable retirement.

What if I was able to alter your thinking when it comes to your money? Test the principals and formulas I write about and see what happens. The only thing you have to lose is more of your hard-earned money!!

0

If your net worth is zero, is it possible to retire a multimillionaire? How do you build wealth and build wealth that lasts? How do you build wealth that transfers to the next generation? How do you build wealth that can be used to help others improve their lives?

HALLS OF IVY

Not everyone will be able to go to college and get a degree that will take a lifetime to pay off. Even if you go that route, it is not guaranteed that your dream job will be waiting for you when you graduate.

Why does everyone rush to put such an emphasis on going to college? My son will have the chance to go to college if that's what it takes to train him for the career he picks. I'm not against it, but I am against the outrageous cost associated with any college degree that will take a lifetime to pay off. How many graduates are using their degree in the career they picked. A high percent of graduates say they are unsure of the value of their degree. So why do so many students see this as their only way to make a good living?

1st Generation Rich is my title for this reason. I saw my best friend's dad build an empire from scratch. He did it with no help, no college degrees, and no safety nets to catch him if he were to fail. His story was so impressive. It motivated me to begin my personal journey. I began searching and digging, and I found out how he was able to take such a simple idea and turn it into a pot of gold. He built a very large cash machine that paid him twenty-four hours a day, seven days a week, 365 days a year. This provided him and his family many great options that gave them all true freedom.

LOOK

Sometimes the simplest ideas are right in front of you. Are you willing to take the time to look? Just open your eyes. Wealth is floating all around you. What does it take to find your great idea? Can you stick to it until success starts popping its head up?

Once you learn these principles and start applying them to your journey, the only thing you will regret is not starting earlier.

PURSUIT

My main goal was to have a thriving business that funded all our investments and pays us every month to live the lifestyle that fits us. I wanted to show others that anyone can reach their goals when they master the financial tools that are available to everyone.

If someone with my background can become 1st generation rich, then everyone has a great chance of being successful. I succeeded because failure was not an option. I worked hard and saved even harder and the results were the only proof I needed to keep me pushing forward.

I'm not trying to reinvent something that has been taking place for thousands of years. I'm simply taking something that was always there and giving you my personal insights of how we built our business and real estate portfolio from the ground up with a very small savings account, no financial help, and no safety nets to catch us if we fell. This made us pay attention to everything we attempted with great detail. We learned as we went and decided that failure had no place in our journey. We stuck to our vision and never stopped until we completed what we set out to do. Then we went on to our next great goal.

ENDGAME

Once you reach your main objective help others find the path that brought you there. Plant a seed by your incredible story. Share with others your knowledge and personal insight of how you were able to **stay** on the road that's less traveled to become 1st generation rich.

A DIFFERENT APPROACH

Have you ever read something that's so incredibly potent you wish that all parents and teachers thought like this?

A principal wrote this letter to the parents of his students:

> Dear Parents,
> The exams your children are about to start soon. I know you are all anxious for your children to do well, but please remember, among the students, there is an artist who doesn't understand math. There is an entrepreneur who doesn't care about history or English literature. There is a musician, who's chemistry grades won't matter. There's an athlete whose physical fitness is more important than physics.
>
> If your child does not get excellent grades, that's okay!
>
> Please don't take away any of their self-confidence or dignity from them. Tell them it's okay—it's just an exam! They are cut out for much bigger things in life. Tell them—no matter what they score—you love them and will not judge them.
>
> Please do this, and when you do, watch your children conquer the world.

One exam or a low grade won't take away their dreams and talents.

And please, do not think that doctors and lawyers are the only ones out there who make a lot of money.

"You can't predict the future, yet your choices can."

INTRODUCTION

DON'T SPEND ANOTHER DAY BUILDING SOMEONE ELSE'S DREAM

Two of the most beautiful words that can change your life are **options** and **freedom**. Having options will give you more choices. The byproduct of multiple choices is freedom.

This entire book from the 1st word to the last word was written with one goal in mind, to show that every human being is exquisitely unique. You were put here on earth for a purpose. I want to help you unlock what makes you unique and turn it into something that lasts.

Each chapter in this book is a steppingstone towards building a rock-solid foundation to launch your ideas from.

If I could show you it's possible to be in control of your future would you believe me?

The most powerful word you take for granted is **choice**. Your choices are great indicators of where you will end up in the future. How can you tell the choices your making now are the right ones?

What can you gain? Satisfaction of ownership. Having money producing assets. Control of your valuable time. Having a fully funded retirement. The freedom to do whatever you want.

What can you lose? An unfulfilling, lifeless job that has no room for advancement. Dealing with grumpy bosses and unhappy coworkers. Another day spent working to build someone else's dream instead of yours.

I will show you the path we took that lead to our freedom. Once you master the principals and engrave these formulas in your mind the next step is to stay on the path until you complete your goals. Once that happens you will be on your way towards becoming 1st generation rich.

> **Realize that your time on earth is short. Why settle for mediocrity when you could have a chance at greatness.**

"Never Accept Mediocrity as Being Great."

PART I

WHO ARE THE 1ST GENERATION RICH?

So, who are the 1st generation rich? By in large, the wealthy have worked for their money. Roughly 80 percent of millionaires in America are the first generation in their families to become rich. They didn't inherit their wealth; they earned it (Cato Institute, Nov. 8, 2011).

How did this group of people become rich? What are some of the ways the 1st generation rich made their money? What inspired them? And does everyone possess the same abilities and skills to become 1st generation rich?

1st Generation Rich is about the building blocks we used to build our businesses and put together our real estate portfolio, which led us to become financially independent. This was all done from the ground up with no financial help and no safety net. This whole adventure was inspired by my best friend's dad. He was a 1st generation immigrant from a little farming village in Sicily. He went on to build a business and then a real estate empire. He did it all with only a third-grade education. He showed me it was possible to take a different path to wealth, which not many people have traveled on.

My journey started with a goal of becoming rich, and in the process, I found something that was incredibly more valuable than what I thought money was supposed to bring me. These chapters spell out the exact steps and processes that my wife and I learned to get us to where we are.

Unpaved roads are never easy to travel on, but the journey was worth every bump.

RICH

Rich is defined as "having a great deal of money or assets." Let's break this down a little bit more. How much money do you think you need to be rich? At what point can you say, "I'm rich—and I've made it?" Will you ever be able to retire comfortably and not have to worry about money again? Is this fact or fiction?

I read a story about a reporter who asked John D. Rockefeller, "How much money is enough?" He said, "Just a little bit more." At the time, the oil magnate he was the richest person on earth.

An old proverb says, **"Whoever loves money never has enough; whoever loves wealth is never satisfied with their income."**

So, is it all about having large piles of cash in your bank account? Is it the quality of life that comes from having wealth? Everyone has a completely different view of what being rich is really about.

BIG MONEY

On a sunny Saturday morning, I decided to play a quick nine holes at a public golf course and was paired up with a nice guy who had the same idea. After we played the first hole, he started talking to me about how he had retired early and lived in this great big house and drove to the golf course in his BMW convertible. He went on to brag about how he made *big* money in the stock market. He stated, "It feels great to be rich," and, "Not too bad for a poor boy from Alabama." After listening to this guy's "I'm rich" stories for the next few holes, I decided to ask him to define what *big* money meant. He looked at me with this extremely large smile on his face and said nothing. That ended his brag-a-thon.

When we finished the round, I watched him slip away and get into an old, broken-down, paint-faded 1990s BMW convertible. It was worth about $4,500 and badly need of a new set of tires. I'm pretty sure he would have had a hard time passing the state emissions test due to all the white smoke pouring out his exhaust pipe.

I guess we all have different ideas about the meaning of *big* money.

> **Being rich is an idea. Being rich is a thought. An idea with no intent is idle. An idea with purpose is life changing.**

REAL RICH

Accumulating more moneymaking assets will create more *options* for us. Having options is what gives us true freedom. We put our money to work so we don't have to work as hard for more money. We built a great moneymaking machine that produces an income while were sleeping.

Three of the things I equate rich with are options, time and freedom. More wealth creates more options. Having more options will create more freedom and more freedom buys you more free time, which means you can make more decisions and not have someone else making them for you.

Wealth = Options + Time and Freedom

When you give yourself more options, you end up with more freedom. When you have more freedom, you have more time to do what you want, to look for more investments—and you never miss any opportunities that might have passed you by. Wealth buys you a lot more than just your toys.

The 1st generation rich have the great task of figuring this all out from the bottom up.

Be the first person in your family to break the mold of the lifeless, dead-end job—and start something that will ultimately reward you with true riches, options, and real freedom. Come to the realization that you were put on this earth to succeed. **The only roadblock that can get in the way of that is you.**

The thought of opening your own business, being your own boss, and making the rules might seem unattainable to some, but people start businesses every single day. What does it really take to get your ball rolling? How do you start something from nothing and build a legacy that gets passed down to future generations?

STEERED IN ONE DIRECTION

Graduate from high school, you pick college, get a degree, and work for someone for twenty-five years in the hopes that one day you might be able to retire? Why do most people pick this path?

What about trade schools?

Why are we only told to study hard and go to college—only so we might be able to work for someone who started a business. What's wrong with the goal of being the one who starts the business and hires those who went to college? How about going to a trade school with the sole purpose of picking a trade to start a business from?

Trade schools cost around $35,000, which is less than the

$125,000 and up for a bachelor's degree. Use the money you save to help launch your new company. Buy a franchise and grow it into multiple locations. Look for any type of business venture that will make enough money and buy you enough time so you can spend your time looking for other investments to own.

WHAT'S YOUR QUALIFICATION'S?

Do you feel your not really qualified by the world's standards? What is the difference between intelligence and knowledge?

A List Apart says, "Knowledge is a collection of skills and information a person has acquired through experience. Intelligence is the ability to apply knowledge."

According to the Dailyherald.com:

> College doesn't make you smarter, study finds. You are told that to make it in life, you must go to college. A study of more than 2,300 undergraduates found 45 percent of students show no significant improvement in the key measures of critical thinking, complex reasoning and writing by the end of their sophomore years.

There is a bumper sticker that says, "Well, another day passed, and I did not use algebra once!" Unless you are an engineer or in a few other careers, that would be pretty much fit all of us. We all learn things we will never use in life. College and algebra did not seem to be anywhere close to what I would be doing in the future. My future looked more like a minimum wage type of job.

I was told on many occasions my future would be bleak without a college degree. Without a college degree, I would have no chance of ever having a real career or salary. Even when I first started my business, some of my clients asked if it was just something I was doing to pay for my college tuition. I always thought this business was going to be my career.

Never listen to the naysayers. Their opinions don't count.

> **A naysayer is a person who criticizes, objects to, or opposes something.**

STARTING INSTEAD OF FOLLOWING.

Someone must be the first. The first one in their family to break out of the normal nine-to-five job to start their own business and begin investing. The first one who started something from nothing and made a living from it. The first one who said they were not going to settle for a dead-end job they had no passion for. The first one to go on and create a legacy that can be passed down to future generations while leaving a unique fingerprint on this planet—a masterpiece made from ideas and perseverance.

1st Generation Rich was written for those who always wanted to start a business and start investing in real estate but have no idea where to begin.

Many people ask, "How did you start your business? How did you get into real estate investing?" I answer these questions in steps. This is my simple, boiled-down approach to how I got started and took it to the next level with my wife. We knew what an opportunity looked like and found the finances to complete the deal. The main goal is to build a moneymaking machine that pays all your expenses and buys you the time to research and search for more deals to own. The more deals you do, the more time you create, which gives you more options to choose from. The by-product of options is having more freedoms.

WHAT'S THE CHANCES?

You can start from zero—with no money and no help—to build a business, invest the profits in real estate, and then invest in other areas.

If the words, **lazy, quit, stop, and I give up** never enter your mind then I would say your chances are good.

Over time, I realized this whole venture had nothing to do with trying to become superrich. Instead, it was all about creating multiple *options* in my life. It was the options that equaled true freedom. Options came because of the way we decided to do business. Having multiple options gave us more control of the decision-making that opened doors to the next great opportunities.

> **An opportunity is a set of circumstances that make it possible to do something. Options are best defined as things that are or may be chosen.**

I don't claim to know everything about business and investing, but I'm an expert when it comes to how we did it. The habits, sayings, and methods I write about work—and the outcome was the proof.

We built options in our life that would not have happened if we had settled for just any job. We took a different path to success. We took a road that seemed to be less traveled due to fear and societal norms. Schools left this important segment out of their curriculum. No wonder this other path is not being used or even looked for. Most people don't even know it exists. Get your degree, go look for a job, and good luck with all the student loans! Most people head down this path. This seems to be the road that's most traveled, and it works for some—but not for all. What happens to all the students who don't fit into that category? I was that student.

1st Generation Rich is a guide that anyone can follow to find opportunities where businesses can be formed, and needs can be met by you and your great ideas.

THERE IS NO SUCH THING AS AN ACCIDENTAL MILLIONAIRE

No one just stumbles upon wealth. Wealth is being made all around us all the time. How do you create a net that grabs some of the wealth? Positioning yourself in the right place at the right time with plenty of cash is one of the winning combinations that creates rich opportunities.

Most people will never have any extra money to invest. They go on living just like their parents and grandparents did. They work from nine to five on Monday through Friday and use the weekends to play and catch up. They stay with the same job—like it or not—until they can retire with some help from Social Security. Most people don't have a problem with that. It works—and it is what it is.

Then there are others who don't quite fit into that group. They picture themselves going down a different path toward success. They dream about owning a business, making deals, buying investments, and helping others along the way. I wrote *1st Generation Rich* for that type of individual. They picture themselves building something instead of just showing up to work somewhere because that's what you're supposed to do. This book is for the person who is working toward ownership instead of just employment. They are going to do whatever it takes to thrive and then profit from making smart financial choices.

Everyone has this treasure chest buried somewhere on their property, but most people are not motivated enough to go looking for it. Life, your own doubts, your so-called friends, and even some family members are some of the reasons your treasure might remain hidden from you forever.

This book is a guide to help you to discover your treasure. It will help you look at your work and your career choices from a different point of view. It will shine a light on a different path. This path might seem hidden because not everybody's looking for it. You might not even know anyone who is on this path. Why do some people find it and become extremely successful when others could care less or even give any thought to it?

We tend to follow what we're taught or what we perceive as safe and logical. We take notes from the people who have gone before us, including family members and friends. That usually keeps us glued to the idea that we think has the best chance of working. Safety, security, self-insurance, and consistency keep everyone moving the same direction on the same path.

Almost everyone in my immediate family found a job or a career and worked until they were able to retire. However, that was not even an option for me. If I really wanted to find true freedom, I had to find another path.

GET RICH STEADY

This is not a get-rich-quick book. It's a get-rich-steady book with the goal of creating options in your life that will guide you toward becoming 1st generation rich. The 1st generation rich are the ones who started with nothing and ended up building businesses that generate a good income. That income can be used to make investments that send you money every month. That's the goal and the endgame.

This book provides insights into our personal journey and explains how my wife and I set goals, examined our behaviors, saved, and invested to give us the best opportunity for success. You will see the process we went through, how we put our deals together, and most importantly where the money to do these deals came from. There is no real secret to becoming 1st generation rich. The real secret is seeing what others seem to have missed. We looked at creating an income from a different point of view.

If you bought this book thinking it was another book on how to get rich quick, you might want to locate your receipt and try to get a refund. You're not going to find those types of hyped promises in these pages.

Sure, there are a couple of ways to get rich quick. Let me think for a second. You could win the lottery. You have 1 in 175 million chance of winning—good luck with those odds. Every week, millions of people spend their paychecks trying to find little shortcuts to become overnight millionaires. You might find yourself believing in something that you think will be the answer to all your money problems. Your money problems are the symptoms of your behaviors.

LUCKY YOU

Our story is proof that luck had little to nothing to do with what we did. Luck played a very small roll in our journey. We just learned how to position ourselves in the market to give us the best chance of having good fortune and having great opportunities find us. We prepared ourselves so we were able to make investments at the right place and the right time and for the right price—and making sure we had plenty of cash to do it.

Just about anyone can do what we did, and people can do it better and faster than we did. We did not become accidently rich. We set out with lots of determination, focused direction, big dreams, and even bigger goals. We took daily actions to make it all happen.

This book is all about the business and investing experiences we used on the entrepreneurial side of the world. This world is not taught in most schools.

This book is the basic, boiled-down approach to how we found success in business and investing with no help from a single soul. It was on-the-job training.

We had no financial help from family or friends. As my grandpa would say, we did it "from the bottom up." We started with absolutely nothing and built a successful business that supplied the money to put together a large real estate portfolio and invest in the stock market. We now have many types of income streams that keep us well diversified.

This is our journey. Our life experiences and truths inspired us to stick with our goals until we started to see success.

BLANK RESUME

My wife and I did not begin our journey with expensive college degrees. I was a community college dropout, and I hired April to work in my growing company before she finished her degree. By not starting with any debt we were able to immediately start funding our **new savings account.** We knew this was the fuel for our investing future. Now we just needed to find the right investment to do it with.

Each chapter in this book will show you the techniques we used to position ourselves to take full advantage of up and down real estate markets and new markets that were popping up all around us. Right now, is one of the greatest and easiest times to start a new business. We have more information and tools at our fingertips than any other generation. You can sell our great ideas to the entire world—and not just locally or regionally anymore.

Starting a business might not be for everyone. You can go to college, get a degree, end up with a great job you love, and still apply the techniques we talk about in this book to find the right investments to fit your personality. Even if you're not an entrepreneur, you can learn how to invest. However, to truly taste the options and freedom that self-employment brings, you'll have to approach your career choices from a slightly different angle or perspective. You're the boss, you make the rules, and you get to make all the decisions. You're the dictator of your own valuable time and energy, and you can construct something that you personally own and believe in.

The goal is to create large intervals of time by correctly leveraging other people's time. Being able to work with different personalities is the most important formula for success in any type of business. This is the fastest and most efficient way to buy yourself time to build your business.

This book will push you to find your niche in the world of business and investing. The ultimate goal is becoming 1st generation rich. You can be the first one in your family to build a multigenerational wealth machine that can be passed on. You can create something from nothing—and then build your own empire. You, your family, and your friends can all benefit from the decisions you're going to make. Why not give it a shot? What do you really have to lose?

R.I.P

Some graveyards are full of missed opportunities and ideas that never had the chance to become reality because of fear, doubt, lack of motivation, substance abuse, or unhealthy behaviors. Some missed opportunities were due to not having any extra finances because of bad planning. Hundreds of other distractions can keep people from truly reaching their goals, which might have been easily obtainable. Don't get stuck following that crowd. Take a different route.

You have an opportunity to invent your entire life from beginning to end. Find out what you can end up creating. Having the freedom to get you there is the most important part of the journey.

The trick is to try. Give it a shot. Go for it. We all need a plan, a little encouragement, and a swift kick in the pants to help us get moving in the right direction. This book includes the steps I used when I started out and the things that motivated my wife and me to keep going. I also wrote about some of the failures. It was not easy street all the time. There were a lot of ups and downs. We made many mistakes, but we kept on learning. We continued on the rocky, untaken path until we figured it all out. We had no one to help us, so we had to figured most of it out on our own.

Every mountain we climbed gave us the confidence we needed to get over the next mountain—and then a funny thing happened. As we became more confident, the mountains started to look more like little hills. Our perspective started to change. What seemed impossible became quite manageable when we decided to keep on pushing forward and never give up. We had nothing to lose and nothing to fall back on, which pushed us ever harder to make things happen. It was do or die trying, and we pushed forward at all costs. In business, we learned to appreciate the peaks because there's always a valley coming right behind it.

> **Give it a shot. Make an attempt or effort to do something. One-third of your time on earth will be spent working—so why not find something that excites you when you wake up on Monday morning?**

THE GREATEST TOOL

This adventure starts the day you begin to understand and learn the uses and influences that come from having access to the incredible tool called money. This tool must be used properly. It is not responsible for its misuse; the problem is the person who mishandled the tool. When I purchase tools, they come with instructions. The written information shows how to properly handle the tool. Money also has a specific set of directions. These are the most underread instructions that ever accompanied an important device. No one seems to have any interest in reading these life-changing instructions. Very strong emotions are tied to this tool. Which can make it hard to understand its functions. Emotions drive most of our impulses and actions. Without a clear, defined set of instructions, it's easy to make a mess.

We used this set of instructions to change our perspective on money. I researched and studied money's instruction manual to really understand the use of this tool—and the function and freedom that come from mastering it.

From the cradle to the grave, everyone is in some way dependent on money. We all use money on a daily basis and probably don't give too much thought to it.

> **Money is limited until you learn to release its potential to become limitless.**

The function of money should not be confused with the love of it. Money should never be stashed due to fear; it should be spread out wisely in different asset classes with an anticipation of a return and appreciation on your investment. Money is a tool that should be taken seriously and used carefully. Money needs to be respected, appreciated, and valued for what it is.

Misused money can bring a load of stress and anxiety in your life, but money handled correctly will open up areas in your life that you had no idea even existed. Money can be a great reward or a curse.

Of course, like anything new, there is a learning curve when it comes to money, business, and investing. No one learns everything overnight—so be prepared to be patient, flexible, calm, undistracted, and willing to give 110% of your energy, time, attention to learn about it. Over time, you will see all the real benefits money can provide besides making enough to just squeeze by every month.

This great journey begins with you and your great ideas. You will end up working in a way that will be completely different from how you thought you were going to earn a living. When this idea about money takes hold—and you decide being 1st generation rich is going to be your path—you will have just entered the get-rich-steady plan for building wealth. By using your income, leverage, patience, and time, making a plan, setting goals, and seeing them all through is the first step on the path to true options.

The only way you can fail at this is if you decide to give up.

Money offers higher-quality health care, food, housing, and lifestyle. You can help other people financially when you see a need. Also, you'll be able to give your time generously to volunteer or mentor. It's a lot easier to do all of this if you master one of the greatest tools that everyone will have access to.

The entire world revolves around money. After your relationships, money comes in close to second place. If something is that important, shouldn't we spend more time trying to learn about it and becoming experts at using it? Unfortunately, if you mistreat or misuse your money, it will ultimately turn on you. Through bad debt, overspending, and no savings, a lack of money will put you in a hole that could take years to get out of. It may even bankrupt you. The stress it creates affects everyone around you.

Money has power. Money is one of the top reasons for divorce. Why do you think that is? There might not be enough money—or one spouse is overspending it. Just the way 2 different people look at their money can create friction. Money mismanagement is powerful enough to rip a marriage apart, creating deep wounds in people.

GREED: IT IS A SELFISH AND EXCESSIVE DESIRE FOR MORE OF SOMETHING THAN AS NEEDED.

Since the 1st generation rich start with little or no money, greed won't be much of a problem in the beginning. As time goes on pay attention to **GREED.**

When you start actively paying attention to money, it is going to be the greatest indicator of your personal success or failure. Learn both sides when it comes to positive and negative ways of handling your money.

PERCEPTION

How do you feel about money? Our emotions usually drive our spending habits. Some people have such a strong emotion toward money that they begin to hate it. They are afraid it is the reason for all their troubles. Almost all money troubles are self-inflicted. Think about it. Who forces you to spend your money? Who pulled your credit card out and swiped it? Who's really in charge when you find something that you just have to buy?

Look to the future with your money. Thinking about the long term when it comes to your money will help you spend in a way that benefits you and does not burden you. The way you treat money will shape the way it interacts with all the aspects of your life—from top to bottom and from the inside out.

Short-term thinking is just going to work for a paycheck so you can fund your immediate lifestyle, repeating the same routine over and over until something unexpected happens or breaks down. Then you try to put a patch on it by paying for it with one of your five maxed out credit cards. That is no way to get ahead in this game. Once you start going in that direction, it's hard to find the extra money to pay it off. The hole becomes a little bit wider and a couple of inches deeper. Before too long, you'll need a ladder and a second job to get out of your mess. This creates a mountain of unnecessary stress that effects everyone around you.

PREPARE FOR REPAIRS

You will always have something break down, stop working, or needing to be replaced or repaired. Your savings is the insurance policy. Always be ready with savings to pay for your repairs. Self-insure because you can bet that these unfortunate breakdowns will eventually track you down. They will find you—they always do.

Focus on your income, pay constant attention to you spending, and actively send every extra dollar you make right into your **new savings account** (explained in chapter 4). Constantly work on building up your balance until you're ready to invest it.

Think about what your money should be doing for you instead of what your going to buy next with your money. Your money needs to be saved and put out on a mission. Give your cash the fighting chance it needs to multiply.

> **Frugal means sparing or economical with regard to money or food.**

Frugality is not a cuss word. Actually, it's more about restraint. It's a mind-set. It's a way of thinking that gets you actively paying close attention to how you interact when it comes to making prudent purchases.

Frugality is not to be confused with being a cheapskate or a tightwad. I consider those terms cuss words. Unfortunately, when I met April, I was a cheapskate. I embarrassed her when I left what I called a tip. It resembled the coins you used to buy gumballs with. There were many times she wanted to leave the restaurant before I paid the check. Over time, I learned to be frugal instead of cheap. Frugality helped us build a large saving account to invest with. Frugality is what led us to being generous with others. Frugal thinking builds up your savings. Rash or emotional spending will do the opposite.

We try to be careful caretakers of every dollar we make, and we always account for each dollar we own. When it comes to spending, it's all about the micro details. You must pay close attention. Money disappears if it's not carefully watched. It can wander off without you even knowing it.

MONEY AND SCHOOL

> **Primary education was designed for general knowledge such as arithmetic, reading and writing—not wealth creation.**

Where are the entrepreneurship classes? We were getting ready to send our son to high school. After looking at all the classes, I noticed his school did not offer anything to do with any entrepreneurship programs. Why not! How is anyone going to learn about starting a business or investing? No wonder everyone is led towards one direction. What's the problem here! Everyone loves choices why not give them an entrepreneurial option?

> **Larry Alton with Inc.com wrote that 66 percent of millennials want to start their own business—and Gen Z is projected to be even more entrepreneurial than that.**

Why don't schools offer these types of programs if there is such a demand? Most students are being pushed to go right in a college program. They end up with a degree they might use and a load of student debt.

The real use of money was never taught to us in school. I assume that's why so many people have such a hard time dealing with their finances when they graduate. Maybe you took a basic economics class in school, but that's exactly what it was (basic).

Do high schools even offer any entrepreneurship classes? Mine didn't. How does anyone really learn about money and investing? Most of us inherit the habits from our parents or the people we are around the most. If you learn the habits from people who also never learned about money, the cycle continues. That's why so many people have bad debt or loads of credit card debt and are living paycheck to paycheck. They never learned to see money as a great tool; instead, it's viewed as just some green paper to buy stuff with.

PERSPECTIVE

1st Generation Rich was written for the person who has no idea what their future could look like. It was written for the person who is stuck in a dead-end job and feels like they have no options or direction. It was written for the stay-at-home mom who is trying to earn an extra income. It was written for any person who thought running a business was what they were made for. It was written for anyone who wants to step out and take a shot at building something by using their passions, uniqueness and great ideas.

Savings and time management are some of the most important components of our foundation. We built our businesses on them. If you can master these two components, you will give yourself a big head start when you decide that nothing can keep you from becoming 1st generation rich. Without mastering these two building blocks, you're most likely just dreaming.

Literally anyone can combine these ideas I write about and turn them into something great that fits their character. Everyone has great ideas from time to time. Some of these ideas will change the world, and some just make for great fun. Awaken the entrepreneur that is sleeping in your mind and see what can happen.

With some planning and self-control **(behavior modification),** you will have a good chance to be able to retire comfortably, wealthy, with lots of options that will give you plenty of freedom. Instead of waiting for a promised inheritance from some rich uncle that might never happen or a lottery windfall, you can begin building your own legacy by building an empire for yourself and your family.

THE SWEET SPOT

Most people are hard at work, working for their money, because that's what we're taught to do. This other group of people comes along and figures out how to have their money work for them. That's the sweet spot! By training your money to multiply, you build true wealth. If done correctly, you'll be on your way to joining this proud group of entrepreneurs called the 1st generation rich.

In the chapters to come, I will explain in detail exactly how we did it. Start projecting yourself into some of these scenarios. Place yourself in the middle of the stories. Wrap your mind around these simple ideas about money, savings, investing, and building a business. Once you realized it could be done, the next step is you going out and doing it.

> **How important are your words?**
>
> Words are singularly the most powerful force available to humanity. We can choose to use this force constructively with words of encouragement, or destructively using words of despite. Words have

> the energy and power with the ability to help, to heal, to hinder to hurt, to harm, to humiliate and humble.[1]
>
> Huffington post, December 15,2014

Research shows that we hear between 20,000 to 30,000 words during a twenty-four-hour period. Over time, we can lose the true meanings of those words. Some of the interpretations get watered down over time.

I include the meanings to show the significance of the words that were important to our success. Hearing was never as powerful to me as seeing. Hearing goes in the left ear and sometimes comes out the right ear. When I see something, it usually sticks with me. I have always been a visual learner. Show me a picture or a graph or tell me a story—and I'll never forget it. I must work three times as hard to retain new information, but once it sticks, I can run with it and master it.

A lot of my learning disability has to do with my memory. I always felt like I had a very finite amount of storage capacity when it came to my mind. I decided to fill it with only the greatest, most dense, most refined, most powerful, most filtered information on a few topics that could easily attach to my memory. For me, it was better than having millions of little useless sound bites bouncing all around. It's got to be black and white; I don't have much use for the gray. Let's get to the bottom of this and move on is my attitude. Just show me how it works; with a little practice, I'll be doing it soon. I overcame most of my shortcomings by focusing on my strengths.

I read an article on WebMD that said, "Your brain has only so much storage space. It needs to make room for new, useful items. And to do that, it must get rid of less important details, as well as those that you don't call on often."

YOUR DAILY GRIND

Life will get in the way of your goals. That's 100 percent guaranteed. Learn the meanings of the words that inspire you. Write down the definitions that give your business and investing ideas purpose. Post your goals on a door you look at every day. Think about your future every day; it's right around the corner.

When you're feeling unmotivated—and you will feel that way—look back at the definitions and goals to remind you why you started this journey in the first place: to become 1st generation rich.

DECEMBER 1993. *Me in front of my truck the day I started my business.*

CHAPTER 1

MY HISTORY

SO HOW DOES ALL THIS START?

My pops worked as a sales representative for Wrigley's chewing gum for twenty-five years until he retired. He had a great job. He did not have a lot of stress, and not having his boss hovering around him made it much easier to do his work. My pops could fix and build just about anything he wanted. He was a master carpenter when it came to his hands.

My mom was a stay-at-home mom. She had the most important job of taking care of all of us, and she ran the daily work of managing the household. She always made everyone who came over to our house feel comfortable. She had the gift of hospitality. She is a great host and is loved by everyone.

We kept ourselves busy with a lot of typical neighborhood activities, which were always going on around our block. My brother and I grew up in a blue-collar neighborhood, and I lived there for nineteen years. Like most of our friends, we had a typical upbringing. We only ate at nice restaurants on special occasions. We hardly ever ate any fast food. Why would we when my mom was such a great cook. The only time we received gifts was for Christmas or birthdays. We were on our own for anything besides the necessities. That's pretty much how it was.

DISQUALIFIED FROM THE TRADITIONAL CLASSROOM

On a sunny morning my second-grade teacher handed me a large brown envelope full of papers and said, "Take this to your parents and don't lose it."

I gave the envelope to my mom. The envelope contained my introductory documents into the Albuquerque Public Schools C-level special education program. According to my test results, some learning disabilities kept me from keeping up with the work my teachers were giving me.

A few major roadblocks in my life made learning tricky. Having been diagnosed with a learning disability and a mild case of dyslexia at age eight made school exceptionally challenging. I had a very difficult time learning.

The next year, I was placed in the C-level special education program. I did not mind the classes because they were a quarter of the size of the classes I was used to. My classmates were all in different grades.

I was in the program from third grade until I graduated from high school. School seemed boring to me, and I was always distracted. Sitting in class for what seemed like eternity made my mind constantly wander off. I started really dreading Mondays after a long weekend, and as the years went on, it got worse. I felt trapped, but I knew I had to complete every year and try to pass with decent grades. My goals were Cs and Bs just enough to get by and not get in trouble with the parents.

As a kid, I dreamed of becoming an astronaut. I thought that going into space would be awesome, but that dream was smashed when one of my teachers said, "You can't be an astronaut because you're not good at math." Thanks for crushing that dream, Mr. Montalto. What an insensitive teacher—but he also was the one who saw all my test results.

From sixth grade until my junior year, I had no idea what I wanted to be when I grew up. I had no dreams and no clear direction. I wandered through school with no goals and with no vision of what my future might look like. The teachers gave me one week to complete the ACT college entrance exam. You know what I ended up getting on that test (saliva.) I was completely bored to death, and I had no idea what any of the answers were. Hours and days of useless questions that made my mind numb. I was completely discouraged and disheartened knowing I was heading for a career that was not going to be too exciting and certainly not involving many options.

When I graduated from high school, I knew college would not be in my future. I'm pretty sure everyone else knew it too. Even the thought of taking college courses was overwhelming. I did not want to pay all that money, especially when I didn't know what I really wanted to do with the rest of my life. It seemed unlikely that I would be able to pass the courses, and it would be a complete waste of my time. Instead, after graduation, I planned to move to New Hampshire to work for my uncle's company.

I planned a trip to Europe for three months after graduation so I could see the real world outside of New Mexico. I was friends with some of the exchange students from high school and would stay with them as I traveled around Europe. Something changed on that long trip. Something just clicked on that trip, and everything reversed. I felt as if I had seen the entire world, and the wonder just left me. I didn't end up staying with my uncle in New Hampshire when I returned. I just settled into my life in Albuquerque and stayed at my parents' house. It was time to finally grow up and get involved in the real world. The big problem was that I felt lost when it came to picking a career because I felt like I did not have many options.

Does every eighteen-year-old know for certain what career path to take—or what they might want to do for the moment or the rest of their lives? That sounded crazy to me. I'm sure some people knew what they wanted to do or at least had some idea based on what other family members or friends had done. I had no vision and wondered what my future could possibility look like.

At the time, I did not know I was going to find a path that was not clearly marked—and I stayed on that path until I join the 1st generation rich.

"You have one life that only you can live. You have the freedom to make it great or mess it up."

SAVE
INVEST
REPEAT

Yes, S.I.R.

CHAPTER 2

AWAKENING: THE DAY THAT CHANGED EVERYTHING

MY GOLDEN TICKET

My best friend, Joseph, lived directly across the street from my parents' first house on Cleopatra Court in Albuquerque. Our moms took Lamaze classes together, and I was born exactly two months to the day before Joseph. We are still the best buds and best friends to this day. Even our kids are named after each other; it was a promise we made to each other in middle school.

Joseph's family was going on a summer trip to Italy, and they asked me to take care of their home while they were away. I agreed and came over to get some direction from his mom. When Mrs. **S** finished showing me all the items on her long list, she said, "By the way, we'll be back in two months."

Two months? I had never heard of anyone going on vacation for two full months. The longest vacation I had ever taken was two weeks. Two full months was unheard of in my circle. I thought only retired folks took those types of extended vacations.

I oversaw his parents' home for the next two months, and my curiosity was suddenly awakened. I could not wait for Joseph to came back so I could pick his brain and find out how his lucky family was able to travel for such a long period of time and not have to work. Little did I know that luck had nothing to do with it.

I knew a few things about his dad. He owned a plumbing company, and he always seemed to be involved in a lot of building projects around town.

From 1986 until 1991, I watched Joseph's family build a large home on two acres of land with an impressive man-made lake in the backyard. His dad was building townhomes, developing trailer parks, and buying vacant land all over town.

I continued to housesit for them every time they went on vacation, and they went on vacation a lot. Questions really started filling my head. Why was Joseph's dad the only one I knew who was investing and building? How come my dad or my other friends' dads and family members were not investing in real estate or running businesses like his dad did? No one in my immediate circle even talked about investing. The questions kept coming, but I never got any answers. Looking back, it was probably because I never took the time to ask them.

THE SIT-DOWN

Joseph's dad and mom were completely self-made. They were truly 1st generation rich. They immigrated from Italy and moved to New York in the 1960s. His dad had no education after third grade. He was a cool, laid-back, easygoing kind of guy. In fact, we gave him a nickname Cool, which fit him perfectly. Cool and his wife Mrs. **S** were the greatest influences in my life when it came time to investing and starting my business.

In 1990, I asked Joseph if he could speak to his dad and see if he was willing to talk to us about how he got his start in business and real estate over a cappuccino and some cake at the Double Rainbow Cafe.

The date was set, and we met his dad at the cafe.

Joseph said, "Dad, Mark and I want to know how you got started in business and real estate investing."

His dad paused, smiled, and said, "Okay."

I found out later that no one had ever asked him that question before. I was kind of shocked. Cool had become so successful, but no one had ever asked him how he made it happen.

For the next two hours, Cool told us everything about coming to this country from Italy with nothing, starting a plumbing company, and funneling all his extra cash into land and real estate. He told us how they built townhomes and developed their trailer parks. The business and investments gave their family the freedom to travel for extended periods of time.

I just listened and took notes. I thought, *If school was anything like this, I would have easily had an A+*. I could not write the notes fast enough to keep up with what he was saying. Cool came over from Italy—not speaking any English and not having any money—and he was able to build something great from absolutely nothing. It just blew my mind.

Those two hours flew by so fast. He had a very simple way of explaining how he started building a steady cash flow from all his properties. He talked about leverage and equity. Those terms were foreign to me at that time, but they would eventually become the building blocks to our own success.

Cool had no idea how much his words influenced my life. He spoke through his actions. I'm forever grateful to him that he took the time to let me peek into his life. That night changed the course of my life forever. Deep down inside, I knew what I really wanted to do: start a business and use the extra money to invest in real estate. That was it! It was so simple and so clear. I now had the perfect road map for how to get there. I rest was up to me.

If Joseph's dad, an immigrant with little formal education, could become super successful without any schooling, I knew I could do the same. All my mental roadblocks melted away that night. I knew I had to give it a shot. Cool's story was so encouraging, and that night was the great turning point for my future in business and investing.

1991

The next year, I turned eighteen. Most of my friends were looking at colleges to attend. College was not even brought up in my home. My parents always encouraged me and never pushed me in any direction. They gave me lots of freedom to make my own choices. I'm pretty sure my parents knew I was not going to be college material. I don't even remember ever seeing my ACT scores. My parents never said anything to discourage me going to college, but they gave me the complete freedom to pick my own path.

I took six-month gap after graduating high school, thinking I was supposed to go to college like every other eighteen-year-old did after high school. I decided to give it a shot in the construction industry. I went to a local technical vocational community college. I was trying to get a two-year degree in the construction industry. I signed up and started on what I thought was going to be my lifelong career choice in the construction industry.

I thought building houses was going to be my ticket to success. How hard could it be? Building homes sounded like a promising future. On the first day of class, I knew I was in over my head. I had no idea what I was about to dive into. It was going to be a lot harder than I had imagined or anticipated. The carpentry classes were easy, but when it came time to take the core classes—English, physics, and civics—the fear crept in. I decided to stick it out. I thought I could possibly squeeze out a passing grade like I did in high school, but I struggled. I felt like I was back in high school. The fear of failure was always stalking me.

I was right. Just like a self-fulfilling prophecy, I was not sure I was going to make it.

My English teacher kindly pulled me aside right before I took her final and said, "Even if you get a 100 % on my test, your grades still are not good enough to pass the class." She was telling me not to waste my time taking the final exam. I appreciated her bluntness, and I decided to drop the class. I was failing most of my other classes as well and decided to drop out of the program completely. That was **not** a tough choice at all. As soon as I dropped out, all the stress I was carrying vanished.

I was an eighteen-year-old community college dropout working at some dead-end job for minimum wage. I figured the construction industry was not going to be in my future. I was lost and wondering what came next.

"Always dreaming without ever achieving is your own fault."

I would occasionally think back to the meeting with Cool and how inspired I was after that life-changing conversation. I wondered what had happened to those dreams of owning my own business and investing in real estate. How was I ever going to inflate these tires, put some gas in the tank, and get this broken-down car moving? That was the lowest point in my life. All of my friends were in college—working toward their degrees and focusing on their futures—and I was working at a sandwich shop for minimum wage with no clear direction. What did the future hold for someone like me who had a difficult time with school and would never have much of a chance of getting any type of education.

I knew that all I could do was keep pushing forward, keep trying, and not give up. That's exactly what I did. I had nothing to lose.

COLD CALL

I was at this party one night and I ran into a friend who said that his new neighbor Zach knew me from high school. I thought it was funny because I had never had any interactions with this guy. I remembered he had a reputation around school for being a great soccer player. On a whim, I decided to look him up, and out of the blue, I called him.

We started hanging out and realized we had similar interests. Both of us wanted to own a business and were interested in investing. I told him I started a couple of small-time businesses in middle school and high school by selling lollipops and flipping Volkswagens. That sparked his interest, which was all it took. Zach and I had the same entrepreneurial itch.

Zach was a lifeguard in an exclusive, gated country club. I used to stop by, and when he got off work, we would drive around the community and look at all the grand mansions that lined the golf course. We always wondered what those people did for a living.

We started bouncing ideas off each other. We were always brainstorming business ideas that we could run together. Zach was just like me two years earlier when I talked to Cool. He just needed a little reassurance it could be done.

THE SEED

Zach's mom was a podiatrist. She brought up the idea that after her single patients had surgery, they needed a way to run errands and buy their groceries. She suggested we start a delivery business to fill the need. We talked about it the next day and decided to give it a shot.

In 1993, we started Road Runners Delivery Service. Channel 13 News did live sit-downs with new businesses and booked us. We did the live interview and started receiving all kinds of calls for yard work, washing cars, and moving heavy furniture. We took every single job and never said no to anyone.

We had a little write-up in the local newspaper under "new startup companies." Within days, we had a message on our message machine. A local advertising agency was looking for a new courier service to do their around-town deliveries. From that one client, we grew the entire business. We began to only do commercial courier services and were able to give up weeding people's backyards. The business grew quickly, and I bought Zach out three and a half years later when his parents wanted him to go back to school to finish his degree.

When we started the courier service, I didn't have much money. I had little savings. I never needed a loan for anything. We saved and paid as we went. As the business grew, I ended up with some vehicle loans—but not much more. I always made sure I had plenty of cash in the bank just in case. I grew the business, watched all my expenses, and was able to make a profit every year.

To follow Cool's advice, I needed to have some sort of income to be able to invest in real estate. I knew the business had a chance of becoming my golden ticket. If I lived under my means, I would have extra money to begin to do what I set out to do when I was eighteen: buy real estate. Get rich steady was my approach. Save, invest, and repeat. Over time, my lifestyle slowly crept up. The more I made, the more options I created—and the cycle continued.

No money equals no investing.

It's that simple! It is not that complicated.

BUSINESS PARTNER/BEST FRIEND

In September 1997, I tagged along with my brother to a local restaurant called Geckos. He was meeting some of his friends for a couple of drinks. Then these two women showed up and joined our group. I recognized one of them from a local café around town. After the introductions, we started talking and hit it off right away. We decide to go a few blocks up the road to a new dance club. After the nightclub, we decided to go to the Double Rainbow Cafe. That was the same cafe that Joseph and I took Cool to seven years earlier.

We had a blast that night, and that's the quick version of how I met my wife. We were married four years later in 2001.

In 2004, April decided that she would become a Realtor/broker. We started DJM Reality. We had complete access to all listings throughout the state and would be saving the 3% commission on each property we bought or sold. We saved thousands of dollars on every deal. She saw that our future was going to be built on real estate, and she decided to take on the job as our broker.

Prime Your Mind.

CHAPTER 3

GET ON THE TRAIN

HOW WE GOT STARTED

How did we start investing in real estate? I absolutely despise making anything more complex or complicated than it has must be. I prefer a simple, boiled-down, understandable approach to everything I attempt. It is very important for me to clearly understand and be comfortable with what I'm about to get into when I get into something new.

When you begin investing, starting small. It's always harder to recover if you go too big in the beginning and end up with a bad couple of deals.

$$$ CAPITAL $$$

So where did the money come from to do our deals? I listen to a lot of interesting investing podcasts, and I read some books about investing. Many of them contain a great wealth of knowledge and inspiration. I love to hear how other investors got started and how they manage to put deals together.

A lot of investors don't tell you exactly how they got the money to do these deals. They can give you a thousand details on how the deal was put together, but they never really tell you how they ended up with the money to do the deals. Why is that? Was it because the money was given to them? Was it an inheritance? Did multiple investors pool their money together? Did rich or generous relatives lend the money to them? It could have been hard work, but why leave how the money was earned out of the equation—especially if someone can benefit from their examples?

I think it's great if you have access to cash through family members who want to help you succeed. You will be way ahead of most of us just by having these options. Most people will never have access to that type of capital. The 1st generation rich have no choice but to figure everything out from the bottom up: how to finance the deals, where the fix-up money comes from and all the other expenses.

As you read on, you will see exactly how we came up with the cash and bought all these properties. There were no complicated tricks involved, and I'll be very transparent about our approach. You will see exactly how we did what we did—from start to finish—and where I hope to be in the near future.

"The future has many exciting opportunities, will you watch others grab them?"

Investing, like everything else, requires time to learn all the rules. If you wait until you're ready, you're never going to be ready. That's normal in the beginning, but as time goes on, you must push yourself to get on the train. Start by reading, joining investment groups, absorbing as many podcasts as possible, and basically doing all your homework. Be ready to recognize a deal. When the deals pop up and the numbers work, you will know it's time to get on board.

TIME TO GO

In 1995, I was living at my parents' home. My mom started dropping little hints by saying, "So, Mark, how many of your friends are still living with their parents?"

I figured it was time to start looking for a place of my own. I started thinking about buying a small house instead of renting. After looking at the rents, I figured I could swing half a small house payment. In 1996, I teamed up with my older brother, David, and we bought our first home together. It was a trilevel home that was in bad shape. It was a time capsule and had not been remodeled since 1960s.

Every dollar I saved in my **new account** went into that house. I finally had my chance to use all the money I had saved for so many years to buy my first real estate investment. It felt great! I was twenty-three years old and owned my first house. We paid $90,000 and put in another $10,000 in fix it up. The remodel was extensive, and everything needed some sort of updating. Everything: Fresh coat of paint, kitchen cabinets, flooring, fixtures, and landscaping. With some much-needed help from my Pops, it took us about four months to complete the home to where we could move in. We had no YouTube videos to watch back then. It was on-the-job training.

I decided that taking on a partner was going to be the fastest way to buy the place due to not having enough money to swing the deal by myself. It worked out great. We ended up with a nice remodeled house that I owned 50% of. We had instant equity because of the sweat equity, and we bought correctly. I bought my brother out a year later when he moved to Portland to work for Intel. I owned my first piece of property and was on my way to becoming 1st generation rich. I was super excited that I finally reached one of my biggest goals, homeownership.

When I bought the house, I knew it was all about the equity—just like Cool said. The equity was going to be the seed to growing our real estate portfolio. I lived in the house for five years before we sold it. We netted $45,000 and banked every penny we made from that sale. The feeling of holding a check for $45,000—and knowing I had done exactly what I set out to do—got me hooked.

April and I decided it was time to buy our first investment property together. We found a bank-owned property directly across the street from my parents' house. We bought it for $115,000 and put $8,000 into fixing it up. I worked on the rehab at night and on weekends. I subcontracted out some of the work and did as much work as I could possibly do to save money.

Fixing it up took up took five weeks, and we had that house rented out two months after we purchased it. The rent always covered my mortgage, and the cash flow was a few hundred dollars. I rented that house out for about a year with no issues. The real estate market was taking off, and we decided to sell the rental. We walked away with a nice $32,000 profit. That makes two and my confidence was on fire. We were on the right track—and we knew it.

WHAT'S NEXT

April and I were driving around the city one day when we stumbled into a brand-new subdivision being built in a great part of town, we both liked. We decided right away to buy a semi-custom home on a great lot and moved into it eight months later. We paid $265,000 for that house. That purchase was a stretch at the time, but we both felt it was going to be a good move. The real estate market was heating up all over the country. It took a while, but the wave finally made its way to Albuquerque. That house went from $265,000 to more than $500,000 in less than four years.

The same builder was also building the exact same home across the river for $45,000 less. I suggested saving the money and still ending up with the same house.

April was adamant about staying on the east side of town, which turned out to be the best move we ever made. Location, location, location—those three words suddenly made sense. My wife's creative ideas and great insight have made us more money. I'm glad I listened to her. The house doubled in price within the next four years due to the real estate market and the great neighborhood.

One of our friends said that we were just lucky to hit such a hot real estate market—and they would be correct in a way. We had no idea the housing market was going to increase like it did—luck maybe—but we still had to position ourselves to take advantage of any future real estate markets, and that is exactly what we did. We had a plan, we saved instead of spending, and we were constantly looking for other opportunities to buy. When we saw the chance to buy, we did not think twice about it.

> **Think about this? You will never build, advance, or do anything by just sitting on the sidelines and watching. You must be in the game to have any chance of winning.**

Get in the game! Imagine if we never took that first small step of buying our first property. Imagine all the opportunities we would have missed if we had sat on the sidelines without taking the time to really learn the rules of the housing game.

You must position yourself so when a deal appears, you will recognize it and be able to financially go for it.

Imagine how much money we would have missed out on if we had not been able to qualify for the third home. That would have been a $235,000 missed opportunity.

At some point, you'll be ready to invest. Your **new account** will be stacked full of cash and ready to go to work for you. You'll know your market and be able to spot a great deal that is loaded with equity. Find your diamond in the rough and buy it.

When you put in the time, the deals will surface. Don't sit on the sidelines and watch other people winning. Get involved, join in, and become one of the players. That's how it works!

SAVE, FIND THE DEAL, AND MAKE THE PURCHASE

After getting our feet wet in the real estate market—and after our first two homes were bought and sold—we became more and more confident. It looked like our future in real estate was on the right track.

We saw another subdivision going up on the west side of town. We refinanced our house and pulled out a chunk of the equity to pay $200,000 cash for a three-bedroom, single-story home. We rented it out for a year. That was one long year. We picked the wrong tenant and paid for it. The rent was always late with a thousand different excuses. They trashed the place and left it a mess. They decided to set up a shooting range in the living room and shot holes in a few of the oversized picture windows from the inside with a BB gun. It took a chunk of cash to get that house back to its original condition. We learned lessons from picking the wrong tenant, but we did not let them discourage us from our real estate goals. We decided to change our investment strategy and get into low- to middle-income fourplex apartments where everything could be replaced for a fraction of the cost.

We decided it was time to sell after one year, and we sold it for $235,000, making another nice profit. Meanwhile, our seed kept growing. We saved and continued to watch our finances closely.

Little did we know the whole economy was about to take a big turn in 2007 About six months after we sold the property, the real estate market started to crash. Now that was luck. I felt like this boom market could not go on like that forever. I was right, and that time, it was luck.

PLAYING IT SAFE

I was playing with my son in the park when I overheard two Realtors talking. They were almost in tears because all their clients were backing out of all of their deals. The buyers were not showing up to the closings. None of their listings were selling like they had been a few months earlier. They were scared to death and thought the market was about to collapse. That confirmed what I was thinking. After a little research, I was convinced that they were onto something. We decided to play it safe and pay off our house by gathering the profits from selling the rental, our first house, and most of our savings and some stocks. We were completely free of debt.

We had no investments and not a lot in savings. We were just sitting on the sidelines because we had jumped off the train. After being on that train for so long, it felt funny to get off and be out of the game. I missed the whole adventurous side of investing, and because of fear, we settled for certainty. I knew we were never going to be rich if we sat there and played it safe while our money was making a very small return with our paid-for house. It was time to open the floodgates.

More millionaires are made during recessions.

That statement did not make any sense at the time. I always thought strong economies made millionaires. That's true if you have all the right ingredients in place to take advantage of a down economy. Buying at the bottom and waiting for it to come back up was our plan. We were about to find out how people became rich during a down economy.

We were living in a great house with no mortgage. Our business was slowly growing. We decided to look on the MLS (Multiple Listing System) on a Sunday afternoon and browse all the different properties that were listed. We decided to look at multifamily properties. Anything from duplexes to three hundred-unit apartment complexes. The properties' histories were also listed on the MLS. We noticed that since the last time some of the properties had been sold, they had lost ten years' worth of equity due to the Great Recession. We knew it was a big buying opportunity. Because of the bad experience with the last single-family home, we said, "Let's give the fourplex market a shot." Middle-to-low-income housing was going to be our new niche.

By having a paid-for house, I realized I was only saving the amount of interest that I would have been paying the bank. The money was just sitting there and was not going to make us rich. We knew we could get a much higher return than the interest we were saving.

With a $251,750 house at 5.5 percent interest and no mortgage, we were saving $1,429.41 per month. We refinanced our home to buy a $179,000 fourplex at 5.5 percent interest. Our payment was $1,016.34 per month. The rents were $2,210 minus expenses, which gave us an average cash flow of $700.00 per month.

We did this again and again with thirteen other fourplexes. The fifty-two units were all providing different amounts of cash every month. Each one was loaded with plenty of equity that we would use to buy more properties in the future. That's the difference between playing it safe with a paid-for house and just sitting on the sidelines or moving to join the 1st generation rich.

OPTIONS!

As we began to build our business and real estate portfolio, we started to notice we were also creating many more options for ourselves. The options gave us more freedom and wiped out a lot of our stress. By having more options, we were less likely to make rushed decisions. The options that came from finding the right deals gave us our true freedom. The options we created were buying us more time to relax and live how we really wanted to. We could simply enjoy the fruits of our labor.

Were we just lucky? We did not sit on the sidelines. We actively jumped into the game and got on the train. We had a plan, we saved, we bought, we sacrificed, and we paid close attention to our finances. We also focused on the market. We made money in a good market and made a lot of money in a down market. Both markets had good deals, and we learned how to find them. We would have been blind to the market if we did not take the time to study and really absorb what was happening all around us.

You must become aware of what the market is doing. Learn terms such as buyer's market and seller's market.

When I was in school, the word *study* sent an uncomfortable, numbing chill down my spine. I hated to study because after spending all that time, I already knew what the inevitable outcome was going to be. That all changed when I found something that gave me hope: real estate investing! All I needed was the time and patience to understand the market and apply my savings to great deals that would pay me back every month.

Thomas Jefferson said, "The harder I work, the luckier I get."

Luck means prospering or succeeding, especially through chance or good fortune. We gave ourselves lots of chances to get so called lucky. We saw many opportunities. Some we pursued, and others we passed on.

Opportunities are circumstances that make it possible to do something.

The economy started booming again, and we found more great

deals to buy. That's because we know exactly what to look for when analyzing a property. The deals are fewer and farther between, but they are still out there. During the recession, we were picking the low fruit—and we knew it. We were buying wholesale and holding, but investors began jumping back in and buying retail, which pushed prices even higher. Everyone has a chance to make money buying real estate if you understand the market. Are you going to watch or partake?

MY PERSONAL DIAMOND IN THE ROUGH

Just about every night April and I would look for houses on the MLS to get an idea where the housing market was going. We always kept an open mind in case we came across a steal. We searched all the properties that had sold within the past year, and I saw what looked like a good trend. Houses were selling closer to asking price, and the listing prices were going up considerably faster than the previous two years combined.

I pulled up every home for sale between $500,000 and $700,000 in an area of town we always wanted to live in. Suddenly, a custom two-story, six-bedroom, four-bathroom home on one acre jumped into my line of vision. It had everything we were looking for—a large three-car garage, a swimming pool, and a great school zone—and it was super close to the mountains. I knew the views alone would make the home more appealing to a future buyer.

The bank-owned property had been on the MLS for about six months. A bank-owned home is usually bought as is. If anything needed to be fixed, we could easily take care of it. Since the home was only eleven years old, it was worth the gamble. The bank had just dropped the price from $636,000 to $601,000. The next morning at eight o'clock, April and I were touring the property. We looked at each other and thought, *I can't believe a custom home with this much potential is still on the market.* We put an offer in that morning for $550,000. The bank countered us at $580,000, and by that afternoon, we had a deal.

Because of the income from all the apartments, we did not have to sell our current home to qualify. That took a lot of pressure off us and made the move a whole lot easier. We closed on Valentine's Day. April used her $17,400 commission to install beautiful wood flooring and repaint the entire house. It was nice to be able to put some of our own personal touches in the home.

After we moved into our new home, we took the tax-free profits from selling our other house and bought an eightplex. The new cash flow easily covered the difference on our new mortgage, and we loved adding eight more apartments to our ever-growing portfolio. We freed up all our equity from the old house and put it to work paying for our new upgraded home in a great sought-after neighborhood that both of us had always wanted to live in. The house had a much better chance of appreciating in value because we bought it at a big discount. We had found another diamond in the rough, and this time, we were going to be able to live in it.

Did we just decide to buy it so quickly because we had a good feeling about the property? No way! We never let our feelings get in the way of any of our decision-making when it comes to buying properties. The key was the months and years of digging into the market, which assured us we were buying a true diamond in the rough. A year later, our home was worth $661,200, and two years after that, it went up to $800,000.

Luck? It sure looks like it from the outside. Luck had nothing to do with it. It was constant planning and patience that brought the deal to our attention.

We gained a very large chunk of equity in a very short period. Due to having so much equity, we did not have to pay PMI (private mortgage insurance), which saved us thousands of dollars per year.

We were able to get a six-figure HELOC on the property and can continue pushing forward with our goals of finding more properties to buy.

Money truly does make money if it's done correctly. Ever hear the saying " the rich get richer". Now that statement makes sense.

Options are the freedom, power, or right to choose something.

Our goal was to have the cash flow from all the properties cover all our living expenses. Once that happened, we created lots of different options. We had the option to choose instead of having someone choose for us. We made the decisions. We move when we are ready. We decide how it will happen and when it will happen. We are completely in control of all the aspects of our lives. It all happened because we planned, took a chance, got on the train, and built a system that provided us with many different options.

Options give you many choices. When you have a lot of options, you will automatically feel the freedom that options create. We could have stayed in our other house for many years. It was big enough for all three of us, but we had options to explore different opportunities because of our investments. When we saw the opportunity to upgrade, we were able to jump on it by seeing the present and future potential value of the new property. Without options, the property would have never crossed my mind. Options gave us the opportunity to find this deal that others might have missed out on.

Having lots of options takes the pressure out of most of the difficult choices we have to make. The main goal is to create lots of options for yourself. By creating lots of options in our lives, we have taken the stress out of so many of our decisions. It also helps us see a lot clearer, and it frees us from fearful decision-making.

I believe it all happened because we set some easily attainable goals. Some critics say you must be in the right place at the right time to be successful, and I agree. If you plan correctly, you will get your shot to be in the right place at the right time. We set ourselves up to spot a great deal and were able to move on it at lighting speed once we found it.

No one knows when that right deal will come—so be ready. If done correctly, you will always find opportunities to create options for yourself. It can be buying real estate or starting or purchasing a business. Will you be able to see it when it comes, and if so, will you have the confidence and finances to take full advantage of it?

Save, Look, and Move

Everyone has the opportunity to do something great in their lifetime. Will you be ready to act when it's your turn?

> **Hindsight is understanding a situation or event only after it has happened developed.**

Unfortunately, we are always just one second in front of hindsight.

Learn from hindsight. History usually repeats itself by leaving you clues. It's a great teacher—apply its lessons toward your future.

Everyone will make mistakes as we branch into area's we are not familiar with, and that's okay! When you are starting out, it's okay to make thousand-dollar mistakes, but try not to make tens of thousands of dollar mistakes, especially in the beginning. Those large mistakes are a lot harder to recover from.

In the beginning never bet all your money on one horse. Never go all in—just in case it does not work out. Play it safe at first; you can go bigger and be more aggressive as you build your confidence and become more comfortable with what you're doing. Start slowly in the beginning, find your sweet spot, and then gradually step on the accelerator.

PRIME YOUR MIND

To start, you need to identify what types of real estate you think you might be interested in. If you're not sure, try finding an owner or investor who owns the type of properties you're interested in and strike up a conversation with them. Find out what got them interested in that type of property—or just find an investing forum online where you can talk to several experienced investors and beginners. Try to get a clear picture of what other people are doing and why they are doing it. Ask lots of questions. Just get your mind moving—and have the mindset like your searching for buried treasure because that's exactly what you're doing.

I thought I always wanted to be a landlord of single-family detached homes. I liked the idea of having one property and dealing with one family. We put our plan together. As usual, it was a simple, uncomplicated plan. We had the down payment and hit the streets to look at multiple properties for sale. The plan was to find an undervalued detached home in a nice area of town that needed a minor renovation. When I say minor, I'm talking about painting, flooring, landscaping, and minor cosmetic remodeling and no structural or roof issues. We did not want to get into a money pit on our first investment because we did not have the extra cash if we ran into too many expenses. We were looking for neglected properties that were not too outdated, and we did not want the expense of gutting the kitchen.

When you close on your deal, the next move after celebrating is deciding how much to spend on fixing up. I took on as much of the work as I could handle. We let the professionals handle everything else. You have access to YouTube and plenty more information online if you decide to take on projects you have no experience in. Be cautious with anything to do with gas or electric. You don't want this to be your last investment.

Be on the lookout for the diamond in the rough. That's the fastest route to accelerate your wealth.

Deferred maintenance with minimal fix-up costs equals instant equity.

Your equity will be the most important factor when it is time to grow your real estate portfolio.

We took our time finding the perfect property that did not need a lot of fixing up. We bought a bank foreclosure—under market value—in a good neighborhood. We did most of the rehab ourselves and subbed out what we did not have time for or were not willing to tackle ourselves. We saved $9,480 in commissions because we put it up for sale by owner. This was all done at night and on weekends while also working ten-hour workdays in our courier business.

The first property got us both hooked on the process. It gave us a real working model for our future projects. Once we got on the train, we had a good idea what to expect.

THE HUNT

Start by searching the internet for different types of real estate investments. You can get an idea of what the market has to offer and how much the properties are listed for by driving around your town and looking at all the different types of properties for sale. Familiarize yourself with your local market and constantly crunch the numbers. Make sure all the numbers work. Look at your mortgage payment, taxes, insurance, utilities, rents, and remodeling costs. Talk to Realtors or property management companies to find out what the properties are selling or renting for in the neighborhood where you want to invest.

I always pick up the free real estate magazines from the supermarket to get an idea about how much houses are selling for when I was starting out. Get plugged in with a good Realtor who will help you understand the market you want to invest in. It helps if your Realtor is also an investor with some of the same investment properties your interested in. You will need to have access to the MLS through a Realtor to really see the details of the property you're interested in. The MLS is a numbers gold mine where the true data comes from.

Look for a true diamond in the rough. A diamond in the rough is something that has hidden exceptional characteristics and/ or future potential—but currently lacks the final touches that would make it truly stand out from the crowd. A needle in the haystack is something that is difficult to find. If these types of properties were that easy to find, everyone would be finding them. Keep pushing forward until you find your gem.

When we are on the hunt for a property to buy, our main goal is to find a property that is undervalued and only needs minor repairs. A Realtor can help you find comps (comparative market analysis). They can easily see what other houses sold for in the area. You can try to find a motivated seller who has to sell the property quickly due to a job transfer, a divorce, or another issue. You can find these deals if you begin to network with other investors or join an investment group. In many circumstances, a homeowner is willing to leave a property or give it back to the bank and walk away. When that happens, be ready to move quickly because you've learned how to recognize a true diamond in the rough.

RISK AND RECKLESS

There is a huge difference between taking risks and being reckless. Being reckless means being careless or being utterly unconcerned about the consequences of an action. Reckless behavior might get you in trouble. Your goal is to be in control of your venture. When you start making smart, calculated decisions—based on what you've learned—it becomes easier to spot a true deal.

Never jump into anything without first taking the time to really learn about it. I read every investment book and article I could get my hands on about the market before we jumped into buying our first property. We bought certain properties because we knew they would work. We never bought hoping it would work out. That would have been reckless.

UNDERSTAND YOUR RISK TOLERANCE

Risk tolerance is the degree of variability in investment returns that an investor is willing to withstand. You should have a realistic understanding of your ability and willingness to stomach swings in the value of your investments. This becomes a lot easier as you gain more experience.

> **The normal human response to the unknown is fear. The best cure for fear is information.**

Make the unknown known by dismantling your fear. Break it down. Tear fear down to its roots. Fear will be normal when you step out of your comfort zone. When you prepare yourself, you will have an idea of what lies ahead. Prep, learn, ask, and talk to other people who have gone before you. Try to get a good idea of what you can expect. Be bold and dismantle your comfort zone. Put your passion in front of your fears and start your journey to freedom.

GETTING STARTED. EVERYONE MUST START SOMEWHERE

A friend of mine wanted to get into the house-flipping business. She found the perfect home for $255,000, and it needed a lot of work. After four months, she had put $165,000 into the renovation and sold the beautiful home for $440,000. She lost money after all the commissions were taken out. She lost money, but she gained a lot of knowledge. You must give her credit for getting on the train. She had an idea and tried it. She did exactly what she set out to do. She lost thousands of dollars—but not tens of thousands of dollars. After that house she knew where she went wrong. Small mistakes added up to thousands of dollars in extra expenses that could have been avoided. I'm sure her next house will be a moneymaker since she paid a few thousand dollars for that education. Learn from your mistakes—don't give up and keep trying.

RISK AND REWARD

Everything we do in life has some sort of risk and reward. You drive to your favorite restaurant and risk getting into a car accident. Have you ever had food poisoning at a restaurant? Do you still go out to eat? What about flying somewhere? The reward is the destination. It's the exact same idea when you start investing or start a business or investing. Find your risk tolerance. Mix risk with a little bit of patience until you find your niche.

The Small Business Association (SBA) states that 30% of new businesses fail during the first two years of being open, 50% fail during the first five years, and 66% fail during the first ten years. With the right business and good timing, there is a good chance of being successful. About 50% of all marriages end in divorce, but every day, people are still willing to give it a shot. That means that 50% of all marriages work out.

Risk is stepping out of your comfort zone when trying something you have never done before. Every new experience will feel foreign until you get used to it, but then it becomes second nature. Your mind loves and needs to be challenged. So challenge it! Build your confidence slowly and expand your talents until you find the business or investment that works in sync with your tolerance for risk. Build upon your strengths and work on your weaknesses every day so you can be ready when that beautiful opportunity pops up. It's always hard to stomach a missed opportunity because you were not ready to act or were unable see it.

OUR FIRST FOURPLEX

When we bought our first fourplex, we had no idea what to expect. We trusted the numbers and felt like we had done our homework, which showed us we had found a good deal. When we were ready to buy a second property, it was a whole different experience. We broke through all the what-if scenarios with the first property. Each purchase after that became easier. When the timing was right, we stepped on the accelerator comfortably buying every deal we could get our hands on.

Risk + Stamina = Rewards

Is there such a thing as being too risky? How do you know when you're getting in over your head? Fear is not always a bad thing. The fear of losing money on an investment will make you dig deeper into the details before you decide to buy. I call that cautious fear. Caution is always good; being fearful is not. Learn the difference.

Risk-taking is choosing a gamble when a safe option is available.

Why not add a little bit of risk into your life? How badly do you want something? You will still have plenty of chances to find your success if something you try doesn't work out. Making mistakes is part of this game. You must go into this knowing that everything, unfortunately, will not always go your way. I've made plenty of mistakes. I looked at each of my many mistakes like I was getting an F on the first exam but ended up with A+ for the semester. You learn as you go. If you have never made any mistakes, you probably have never ventured out of your comfort zone. Some mistakes are just solid proof that your trying.

Leave security, familiarity, and safe place behind for a chance at prosperity and greatness. Don't be the person who said, "I should have." Be the person who says, "I tried it—and I did it." Have no regrets. The only regret you should have is that you did not start earlier.

Risk and reward refers to the possible profit of a particular activity in relation to the risk involved in doing it.

The 1st generation rich's maxim is risk and reward. It might feel a bit risky when you buy your first investment property. You might not know what to expect with all the time, all the money, and all the unknowns. Here are a few words of wisdom to help ease your mind.

- **Never! overpay for a property. Get solid comps. Having equity is a must!**

- **Fall in love with the deal and the numbers—and not the property.**
- **Pay attention to the market you're going to invest in. Timing is everything.**
- **Manage it correctly and profitably.**
- **Never jump in until you're ready with plenty of cash in your new investment savings account.**
- **The numbers will tell you to pull the trigger and do the deal. Don't rely completely on your feelings; they can sometimes be horribly misleading.**
- **Become an expert in the market you're interested in. Read, watch videos, and talk to as many people as possible about subjects you're not familiar with.**
- **Go make it happen.**

When you find the right deal, jump on it—and do whatever it takes to get the deal done.

You might ask, "What is the magic number when buying a fourplex?" A friend of mine bought a turnkey fourplex at full market value. She had a large down payment and was very happy with her monthly cash flow. Her apartment will be paid for in thirty years. As time goes on, she will end up with a nice monthly income, but it might be a while before she sees her equity grow since she bought at the top of the market.

We take a much more aggressive approach. We like to find properties that are in need of work, or we look for bank foreclosures that have a lot of deferred maintenance. We need each of our properties to have a lot of equity so we will be able to get lines of credit on them down the road.

A line of credit is a loan where the lender agrees to lend a maximum amount within an agreed period (a term), and the collateral is the borrower's equity in their property. Equity is the difference between what you owe and what the property is worth.

Let's say you found a deal for $100,000 and spent $15,000 to fix it up. The appraisal on the property comes back at $185,000. You now have $70,000 in equity. The $100,000 purchase price plus $15,000 in fix-up costs minus the current value equals $70,000 in equity.

Deferred maintenance is the practice of postponing maintenance activities such as repairs on a property in order to save costs. When an owner tries to save money by cutting corners or not keeping up with the maintenance on the property, all kinds of disrepair might happen. That's the exact type of property we look for: a property that has good bones but needs a lot of love.

WORKING UP TO A NO MONEY DOWN DEAL.

When buying investment properties, the bank will have you put down 20–30% of the purchase price to secure the loan. Unless you can get owner financing, this is the most common way to buy properties.

Fannie Mae and Freddie Mac were created by Congress in 1938 during the Great Depression. They buy up the mortgages from lenders, which allows them to do more lending. If you finance anything under a five-plex, you will not need to get a commercial loan to do your deal. Usually the loans are thirty-year, fixed-rate loans, and your interest rates will vary at the time of purchase. These loans are great because your payment should be manageable. Fannie and Freddie will let you buy up to ten of these types of financed properties through them, including your primary residence. After you have acquired ten properties, you need to start looking for other creative financing to do your deals—but that's a great place to be.

There is nothing I dislike more than reading something that sounds too good to be true—and upon further examination, finding it is just that. There will always be snake oil salesmen hitting the internet, spewing their lies, and trying to get you to believe in something that only benefits themselves. When I talk about no money down, that's exactly what I mean. It is possible to do a deal with no money down. Let me explain.

To start, you must find the diamond in the rough or someone who needs to sell their property fast at a big discount. You're looking for a property with at least 20–30% equity once it's fixed it up. Here's the part where it might take a little bit of time to get there. The trick is to pay cash for the property.

We have the cash by using our savings, home HELOC and two lines of credit that are on a few of our other properties. In most cases cash deals are accepted faster than regularly financed properties and can close quickly, especially if you're buying a foreclosed property. When the complex is fixed up and rented, you find a lender to put permanent financing on your property. When the appraisal is complete—and if you bought correctly—you should have at least 25–35% of equity in the property. That should more than secure your lender's down payment requirements. When you put permanent financing on your property, you will get all your cash back and all the fix-up money you put into the property, which leaves you with all your funds to do another deal. Doing it this way saves us from having to put $45,000 or $65,000 down to do each deal. Also, by making an all-cash offer, the seller will most likely lean toward your offer—and it might just help you seal the deal when they have multiple offers to look at. Only some of our properties were bought this way. That's how you do it. If the numbers work, pursue the deal.

Because we are 1st generation rich, we did not have anyone to go to who had that type of money to help us do our deals. We worked up to this point. It took us a little while, but once things got going, we found the money easily. Once we financed more than ten properties, we found a lender who did a commercial loan for us, and we only had to have 25 percent equity in the property, which was no problem. The rates were a little bit higher—and the terms were not as good—but it kept us on the train so we can continue to build our profitable portfolio.

Our guidelines for what we will be buying are very specific. We will pass up multiple deals because the pieces do not always fit together. We never buy a property and just hope the deal will work; that is not a good move. We are confident in the deal because the numbers work. The numbers tell us to do the deal. Good, solid numbers will tell you if you have a good deal or one you should pass on.

I always have a difficult time sleeping after we have a signed contract. It is not from being nervous or worried; instead, it's from the excitement of knowing were adding another moneymaking property to our growing multifamily portfolio. When we close, I know that we are that much closer to our goals and that much closer to creating more options. Each property we buy is equivalent to buying more time to do the things that are most important to us. None of this would have happened if we had settled into a normal, comfortable lifestyle and accepting mediocrity as being great.

Position yourself so you will be ready to take advantage of every great investment that crosses your path. When the train leaves the station, make sure you're on it. The hardest part is getting on the train. Once you're on the train, your goal is to advance from economy class to business class and then to first class. Position yourself to one day own the train. Each of your goals should be bigger and better. Set the bar high—and then go for it. Everyone has to start somewhere.

The rewards are monthly cash flow, equity, appreciation, tax benefits. The pride that comes from ownership and controlling of your own future will outweigh the risks.

If you bought correctly, your rewards will soon surface. All the hard work that got you to your first property will make buying the second, third, and hundredth property a whole lot easier.

That's how we did it. We built up our bank account and were ready for the next deal to surface. Money has a way of generating more money if it is invested properly.

> **So, what are you waiting for! Prepare to board your train.**

UNLIMITED CHANCES

The only real and true factor in our success was deciding early on that both of us would never entertain the option of failure. Failure meant we would have another chance to try a different approach by stepping back, reassessing what happened, and trying something else.

> **Failing does not make you a failure; it is the greatest indicator that you are trying.**

You can take the necessary steps toward creating your future, but none of us can predict how it will all play out. By moving in the right direction, you increase your chances of conquering what you set out to do. Patience and constant financial self-control equal investment opportunities over time—not overnight. Stay in the game—you can only do this when you have a passion and a purpose. How bad do you want it!

DECEMBER 1990. *The very first Volkswagon I bought to flip.*

CHAPTER 4

ZERO

ZERO

NO MONEY TO START WITH?

Money is limited until you learn to release its potential to become limitless. Go directly to your bank today. **Open a brand-new savings account**. Every single dollar you deposit into that account from now on can only be used for investing. When I did this, I named it my **"New Account."** I watched it grow, and when the time was just right, I would pull out the money to buy investments that would help me replenish the savings account, building a larger savings that was giving me more capital to go out and buy more investments.

Having a large bank account is going to be as important to you as having gas in your car. It keeps things moving. You must discipline yourself to be a committed saver. By building up your savings, you will be storing up the fuel that will be used to fund your startups, which makes it possible to start investing and keep investing.

Without savings, it will be incredibly hard to get started. This statement almost sounds silly, but why do people have such a hard time with savings?

I'm not even talking about saving large amounts of money in the beginning. It's about gradually building up your savings one dollar at a time. In the beginning, it's not about getting rich quick; it's about getting rich steady.

Every time we apply for a loan to buy a property, the underwriters at the bank want to see how much we have in our savings accounts. They look to see if we have a history of being able to save money. To the banker, it's an indicator of good money management and self-control. You need to prove you're able to pay back the loans, and having a healthy savings will help you do that.

Let's say you can't save a dime. Every dollar you make has a funny way of disappearing. Let me give you a clue to what might be going on. If you happen to explore one of your rooms or the garage, you might see where some of your money is hiding.

"But it's okay," you say. You work hard and deserve every purchase you make. As time goes on, that type of thinking will cause you to miss the **Goldilocks window**, which is the time before life and expenses really kick in. Anyone can start saving at any time. It's never too late to start. In certain seasons in life, it will be a whole lot easier to save. The Goldilocks window is explained in detail in chapter 11.

In January 2019, CNBC reported that 80% of all workers live paycheck to paycheck.

Your goal is to become one of the 10% who save 30%or more of their paycheck each month. If you force yourself to save from every paycheck you earn, it will become automatic when you are making more. Mastering financial muscle memory—just like anything you want to be great at—takes a lot of practice and discipline.

Work should be your best friend and not your enemy. The same goes for saving. Each and every dollar you save will get you that much closer to lasting financial freedom.

We always depend on our savings, and we don't fall behind the ball and have to catch up. When we have a good year and owe thousands in taxes, we go to our savings and take care of it immediately. There is no stress or trying to come up with extra cash. The money is just sitting quietly in our account—waiting to help us.

I'm trying to build a case for all the components you will depend on to carry you to the finish line. If you find yourself spending instead of saving, it will be a lot harder to start. If you learn to practice saving, you will see how a large pile of cash will help ease your financial worries. When your mind is not distracted with financial worries, you can start spending more time focusing and using your mind to create wealth.

It's all about the money. There is no way to build wealth by spending money on things that will eventually take you further away from your main goal of saving and investing.

"To have more, just want less."

Think about that for a minute. Let that statement sink in. There are wants and needs. After necessities like food, clothes, and shelter, everything else is just a want—and I mean everything. There will come a time to buy your wants. And when that time comes, you will have enough money to buy whatever you want whenever you want it.

Savings + time + knowledge = wealth

THE MOTORCYCLE

When I was in the seventh grade, my best friend Joseph had a little 100 cc Honda motorcycle. I saw how much fun he was having on that little motorcycle, and I thought cruising next to him would be awesome. The problem was that I had zero money in my savings account at the time. I was eleven years old—way too young to get a job. Saving Christmas and birthday money was not going to cut it either. Also, my parents were against the idea of me owning a motorcycle. I proposed an idea to them, and I got them to agree that if I came up with enough money to pay for everything related to the bike, then I could go ahead and buy one.

An idea popped into my head. I could sell the large container of leftover lollipops I got as a Christmas gift at school to raise the money. Since I had no other options at the time, I went ahead and started my first business.

At first, it took a while to find my customers, but things began to take off. I kept on buying and selling more buckets of lollipops. Soon I had cases of lollipops all over my bedroom. The school's snack bar held a monopoly on all snacks—so why not give them a little competition? Unfortunately, I found out the hard way that schools have a problem when you're selling the same products at a 50% discount. I ended up in the office a few times chatting with the Principal.

By the end of eighth grade, I had enough money to buy my very own Honda 125 Enduro motorcycle. My parents were shocked when I said I had the money. They wondered where all the money came from. It took me two years to reach my goal—without a job or any financial help. It was a great boost at a young age to know that if I had a goal and saved, I could buy just about anything I wanted. As a little thirteen-year-old, I was driving all over the streets of Albuquerque on a motorcycle I bought by selling lollipops at twenty-five cents apiece. Having that kind of freedom was worth it but cruising next to my best friend was the real prize.

Ideas + goals + saving = freedom.

TIME TO MAKE THE PIZZA

When I was fifteen, I started my first job at a pizzeria. I worked my tail off and hustled every night. I was making minimum wage. For every hour I worked, I was making my boss rich. Of course, that's what I was hired for. He owned me in a sense—or at least he owned my time. I punched a clock, worked, left, and repeated it the following night for $3.15 per hour.

As I was closing the dining room and taking all the trash out, I thought, *Someday I am going to be on the other end this. I'll be the boss instead of the employee.* I don't think it had anything to do with the boss's brand-new black Porsche 911 that he conveniently parked right across from the dumpster.

My boss was opening locations all over town. He was building strip malls where his businesses were located. He was a great inspiration to me. He had the best pizza in town—hands down—for many years.

That was my first job. I was grateful to have that job at such a young age. It was an eye-opening experience. All those employees were working for a great entrepreneur to help him build his brand and make him a success. Why not? He had a great idea. He was a go-getter, and he decided that he was not going to work for someone else. He took the time to create something he believed in, and he made the bold move of bringing his delicious product to the masses.

THE VOLKSWAGENS

As the years went on, a couple of my friends in high school were buying old muscle cars, fixing them up, and selling them. They had older siblings and their parents cosigning the loans for them to buy the cars.

I was not able to afford the muscle cars they were buying since they were way too expensive. I saw this car idea as a great opportunity. I had to get involved and did not want to miss out. I set another goal to find cars that I could afford. I started buying old VW Bugs to fix and sell. I learned how to do the body work, and I found an automotive paint shop to paint all of my cars. They were beautifully done. Every Bug was restored to its original glory. In the process, I was teaching myself business skills that would eventually transfer into my business and investing career.

I restored the Volkswagens for about three years, and I made money on every Bug I sold. I saved all my profits. I also was working a couple of minimum-wage jobs that provided the capital to invest in my new car venture. I was buying and selling VWs all through high school. I also started buying motorcycles, riding them around, and then flipping them. I bought right so when I went to sell, I either made money, broke even, or only lost a little bit. The whole experience was fun. Each time I made a sale, it helped build my confidence. I figured if I could do it with cars and motorcycles, I should move on to bigger goals like flipping houses. The only problem was where was I going to get the money from. No one was going to lend me that kind of money.

How are people working up to buying and selling homes? How does anyone find the money to do it? Getting started is always the hardest part. Something clicked in my head. I figured if I started small, I could slowly work my way up to larger deals. And that's exactly what I did. I built up my new account with one dollar at a time, slow and steady until my opportunity came along.

PURPOSE

When you learn to harness the real power of this incredible tool called money, your life will never be the same.

> **It's not about the love of money; it's about the function of it.**

You need a purpose and a mission to account for every single dollar you touch. Start cultivating a new mind-set about accounting for every dollar you come in contact with.

> "Money never discriminates."

As you become mindful of where each dollar goes, you'll notice your bank account growing. Next, you'll be looking at all your options for investing and multiplying your cash. Take the time to learn about and become acquainted with the types of investments you're comfortable with. When you find one, master it. Once you're an expert on it, broaden your search options and be on the constant lookout for all sorts of different opportunities. Some doors will open, and some will close. Sometimes we look at hundreds of deals before we buy one. We had plenty of deals under contract that fell through.

We just start the process all over again. Stay plugged in until you find the deal that is just right for you.

Patience will create profit and your freedom over time. **Impatience** will ultimately steal from your future. Patience mixed with intention is powerful.

MISSED IT

When your new account is fully funded then the time to jump in is now. Every single day is filled with lost opportunities. If you are not ready to see them or don't have the finances to buy them, someone else will gladly swoop in and become the proud owner of something that might have had your name written on it. Be ready to move on it.

Right now, we are in a great position to buy any type of deal that fits our checklist. I'm looking daily for great deals. We know exactly what we're looking for and what to expect after we purchase. We are just trying to duplicate what we have already done. We intend to go bigger and buy better with each deal we do, branching out one **small** step at a time. I said *small* because this process takes time.

Realize that your success was up to you the whole time! It's right in front of you, and it's been there the whole time. Look for it. Go and find what captivates you. Make it your ambition. Make it happen.

> **Ambition is an earnest desire for some type of achievement or distinction, power, honor, fame, or wealth—and the willingness to strive for its attainment.**

Get rich steady, and one day, you will realize you did it.

Why not take a chance on your dreams? If you're hesitant or have cold feet, that's okay. It's normal until you get the ball rolling. Getting rich steady is a process. It is a marathon—not a sprint. You're the boss, and you're in control of your ideas. Put your ideas to work for you. Turning them into a profit center—one idea at a time.

This journey called life can be exciting and adventurous. It doesn't have to be boring and monotonous. You're given something that could be turned into precious gold; it's called choices. You can select or decide when you face two or more possibilities. Choose something you can see yourself excelling in and having a great time doing. Choose your path to freedom. Make choices that benefit you, your health, your relationships, and your future.

Choose to be the greatest at whatever you do.

PATIENCE PRODUCES PROFIT

CHAPTER 5

THE INCEPTION

THE RIGHT IDEA

Is it really that hard to start a business? The trick to starting something is to just start! That's it,—just get started. Plain and simple. Some so called secrets are so simple that they are not secrets at all. The magic formula is to just get started.

A swimming pool gets filled with one gallon of water at a time.

It's a slow process that will provide endless hours of joy for its users. The same applies to marathon runners; it's one step at a time. All the hours of training, dieting, and planning pay off once you cross the finish line.

The beginning of any business is having **the right idea**, planning, and executing your ideas in the marketplace. What does it take to get started? Start with self-examination. Make a list of your likes and dislikes and your strengths and weaknesses. What are you good at and not so good at? Brainstorm your interests, hobbies, and indoor and outdoor activities. You need to compile a complete and detailed profile of yourself. There is plenty of free information online that can assist you in finding out how you tick. Take that information and apply it to yourself.

I've always liked talking to people. I also liked driving around, and I always wanted to own a business. All I needed to do was find something that fit my personality. A great idea from my friend's mom was to start a courier service. Almost all the components to make this business work were already in place. I just had to figure out everything else as I went along.

Find a need and be the one who fills it or find a way to make something better. That's one way to look at starting a business. Some business ideas will just fall in your lap if you're in the right place at the right time. Others will take time to find.

Be on the lookout for any need that you can fill. When I started my delivery business, there were already plenty of established delivery companies that had been around for a while. I thought, *Why not start one more—but do it better?* None of the other delivery companies were doing any type of work with attorneys. I decided to incorporate legal support to our growing list of services. That's how we found our niche. We put our ideas out in the marketplace and waited for the marketplace to respond. Sounds a lot like fishing. Fishing for clients using great ideas as the bait.

FIRST STEP

Getting started is the hardest part—but just get started.

1st Generation Rich was written to encourage you—the one you out of the billions of people on earth—to explore all the incredible possibilities that are right in front of you and waiting to be discovered. Something clicks in the heads of most entrepreneurs, and the veil of doubt and blindness lifts. Then you're able to see the real capitalist world through the eyes of an entrepreneur. You will become part of this ever-growing machine called business. Your ideas will eventually turn into your own company. Your business will focus on providing exceptional service for your clients while having a great attitude. This is the building blocks for winning in any business. Your attitude will make or break you.

MARKETING

When I go to the hardware store, I always see groups of business cards for plumbers, electricians, and twenty other types of startup companies. They are all trying to get their names out there. I constantly call these companies, and some work out great—and others do not. Some of these startup businesses give me amazing quotes for the work I need done. Suddenly, they have more work than they can handle. They're hiring guys, and their businesses take off. Hard work pays big dividends if you stick to the fundamentals:

- **Show up when you say you're going to. If you say you're going to do something, do it!**
- **Have competitive, fair pricing.**
- **Follow up and deliver the best possible customer service.**
- **Save, save, and save.**

If you start by doing these four things well, you are creating and branding your name as someone who is passionate. It shows you care about the customers and your business. When your customers see this, they will want to help you become successful. That's when a great relationship can form.

"Focus your ideas on a need that the market will be attracted to."

My pops started a handyman service. He put his business cards up on the boards at the senior center. An elderly woman called and needed some small jobs done. From that small job came bigger jobs, and the word spread. Soon, he was booked up doing jobs for all kinds of clients. He made more money in three months than he did in a year working at his other job. The best part is he was in control, and with control come many different options.

He looked at his talents. He always liked building and fixing things. He already had the tools and the knowledge from all the years of working on our house. He had the vision to start a company and provide great service at a reasonable price. All he had to do was find the work. After he was established and because of his perfectionist attitude, the jobs came pouring in. He took a leap of faith outside his comfort zone and made something happen. He found a need and filled it.

Everything starts with an idea; some are small ideas that never take root, and others will go and change the world. The idea is the seed. You need to find some compost for the seed. Any good gardener will tell you how important the soil is for the growth of the seed. The soil is knowledge. Knowledge is the how-to. What does it take to get into this business? Do your homework to find out what steps are involved in launching your idea. If it seems you're having a hard time finding just the right seed or idea to plant, try writing down your likes and talents. Make a long list. Keep looking and writing down ideas that you could imagine yourself doing. Check online to see if someone is already doing it.

You could always investigate buying an existing business or franchise. Once you have picked out your seeds and put them in the soil, the next step is to water and tend to them daily. Tending is looking after your idea, and the water is the cash and time your put back into your idea to make it grow. When you have these components down, you greatly increase your chances for success.

Make sure you do everything possible to make your idea a success. When I started my business, all I could think about was excellent customer service. I always made sure all my clients and customers were satisfied with the service we were providing. If a problem came up, we would do whatever it took to fix the problem immediately. And, of course, the customer is always right.

Have a good attitude when dealing with the people who are paying your bills.

Sometimes you will pick the wrong type of seed and it dies, and that's okay. You can always plant other seeds. Planting a variety of seeds is another option.

A Realtor friend was always trying to start all types of businesses. He tried selling golf clubs online. He even bought a hot dog cart and tried some other start-up businesses that never got off the ground. All of them failed, but he never gave up. He used these failures as learning experiences. Today, he has a very successful line of household goods that he is selling on Amazon. He never gave up. He kept pushing forward. Even when he lost his initial investment on other failed businesses he kept pushing forward at all costs.

Once you find your seed, start by watering it. Without water, your seed cannot grow; without cash, it's a lot harder to fund your venture. You also can bring someone to the table who has the money if you have the idea. I've seen that work out plenty of times. The most important thing to remember when your seed grows is to start harvesting the fruit. Don't hoard it all for yourself—and give some away. Help other people plant their seeds.

When I was twenty years old, I opened a mutual fund with $1,000. My goal was to fund it for twenty years. I figured it was a great way to save each month. I set up the automatic withdraw option, and I had to make sure the money was in my savings every month to fund it. As time went on, I saw that my balance was steadily growing. I enjoyed looking at the account statements each month. It was a great lesson in how the stock market worked. I stayed with it to this very day. That one account grew into several different stocks that have built up over time. It was another asset class I always wanted to get into. I'm glad I did because the banks like to see that you have a track record when it comes to your savings when you're applying for a loan. The money also helps to collateralizing other loans we apply for.

No one becomes an expert overnight with anything. With a few exceptions, most of us learn as we go. Mistakes are **guaranteed** when starting out. No matter how careful we are, we all make plenty of them. Don't let mistakes bully you into quitting. If you feel beat up that's normal. Just don't let mistakes knock you out of the ring.

A mistake is a great teacher who will gladly let you take her class over until you get a passing grade.

Learn from mistakes and move on. There is no need to sit in the same class twice.

When you're starting out with investing, try small investments. The goal is to work up to bigger investments. Play it safe in the beginning to get a feel for how the process works. Once you're comfortable with the process, be more aggressive. There is no need to rush in the beginning. Read, watch, learn, and then do.

IT'S NOT COMPLICATED

Complicated means involving many different and confusing aspects.

To complicate something is to make it more difficult or confusing by causing it to be more complex.

Are business and investing supposed to be complicated? When I'm analyzing a property I'm interested in, I break it down to the simplest most basic components:

- **How much is the property worth now?**
- **What are my estimated loan and escrow expenses?**
- **What are other units in the neighborhood renting for?**
- **What is the estimated fix-up costs?**
- **What is the approximate value of the property when I'm finished with it?**

If you can get a good reasonable idea about these five main ingredients before you sign a purchase agreement, you can rest assured that you made a competent decision. Acquisition costs plus fix-up expenses minus appraised value equals a large amount of equity if purchased correctly.

The same thing goes for business. It's all about the numbers. When buying a business or creating a business, the numbers will give you a good idea if it will fail or be a success. I like keeping things simple. I have no problem asking for help when I need it because no one has all the answers. I try to minimize my mistakes by asking the right questions to the right people.

Keep this in mind and be humble.

You're not an expert yet—so don't try to act like one.

The unknowns can seem overwhelming at times, especially when you're starting out. Take a step back, do some more research on the investment, and crunch and work the numbers. The numbers will tell you to do the deal. When the numbers look good, pull the trigger. Go for it. If you can't make it work, walk away. No one can buy all the deals out there—so wait for your deal to come. Be patient and never stop looking for your next deal.

We have had plenty of contracts on many deals that never worked out. We are okay when they fell through because it's usually a sign that it was not meant to be. It's not a big deal, and we start the process all over again. Having a contract on a property really brings everything to light.

TWO FOR ONE

I was driving around the neighborhood and came upon a vacant duplex that was for sale. I found out it was a bank foreclosure that needed a lot of work. I went to my office and crunched the numbers. All my main ingredients were met, and I knew within twenty minutes that it was going to be a great deal. I put in a lowball all-cash offer at

$75,000. There was no way I was going to lose that one. The bank accepted my offer, and I needed to put down $7,500 earnest money within twenty-four hours. As usual, I was super excited. I knew the property was loaded with equity.

The next day, I was having lunch with a buddy, Big T, and I showed him the great deal that every other investor had overlooked. He looked at the numbers and cash-flow projections, and he agreed that I had found a true diamond in the rough.

That evening, Big T texted me: "Hey, did you realize you are only purchasing one side of that condo?"

Condo! What condo? My offer was for a duplex—not a condo.

I jumped up out of bed and got on the MLS. To my complete disappointment, the duplex turned out to be one condo unit. I had completely misread the legal description and thought it was one plot instead of two. I was about ten hours away from putting down my nonrefundable $7,500 earnest money deposit. Fortunately, I was able to back out of the deal with no issues. I felt foolish for not paying closer attention to the details. I had blinders on because I fell in love with the deal and did not pay attention to the details.

About five weeks later, that single condo unit was pending for $55,000. Two months after that, it was back on the market for $100,000. I was glad to see someone else was going to make some money on the condo. So, at the right price, every property is potentially a good deal. I just happened to miss it twice.

Mistakes are great teachers. After that whole fiasco, I learned to slow it down a bit and pay closer attention to the details of the property, which would have told me that I was looking at a condo instead of a duplex.

LITTLE HELP HERE

Some parents or grandparents have already worked long hours and taken the risks to build a successful business or income-producing investments. If someone in your family took the time to figure out and execute a plan so you could have a prosperous future, you can use their platform to launch your own successful business or investment. My parents did not have a business to pass on. The 1st generation rich usually don't have much of a safety net or help. It's do—or die trying.

This could be a good thing. By not having any backup plan or safety net, you will have to be that much more careful with your decision-making and finances. You have to be that much more in tune with what's going on inside your company. You have to watch every penny being spent. You have to look carefully at every invoice and credit card statement. Every business has problems with cash flow, hiring, or making a profit at first. When mistakes are made, that's when school begins.

Failure is not the end; it's just another lesson that can be applied to your next attempt.

ACCIDENTALLY WEALTHY

The chances of waking up one morning to suddenly find out some rich distant relatives deposited a large amount of cash in your bank account are slim to none. The chances of winning the lottery are 1 in 175 million. Even inheritances get messed up a lot of the time.

If you don't go out and make it happen, assume it's not going to just happen. Whenever I talk to wealthy people, they all seem to have drive, passion, and goals. They have plenty of goals. They all agree it's also about hard work and timing to make the money and buy the assets at the right price. Finding a good deal and buying correctly is one of the fastest ways to build your wealth. Then repeat—again and again.

Anyone can find an investment to put money into. There are investments everywhere. Someone will always be there to sell you something that you might **not** want to invest in. Buying just to buy something is foolish. If you want to really build wealth, you will need to continually find cash flowing investments that are loaded with equity or have the potential for a great return on your money.

PATIENCE PRODUCES PROFIT

> **Patience is the capacity to accept or tolerate delays, troubles, or suffering without getting angry or upset.**

A friend bought a fourplex at full price. It did not need a lot of fixing up, and it was already in pretty good condition. He had a large down payment, and it began producing a good cash flow right away. As time goes on, I'm sure he will end up quite happy with his investment. It's in a good rental area with above-average rents.

He bought this property with no equity in it. He had a chunk of cash and was anxious to buy something right away. His Realtor sold him on this building by saying, "We need to act fast on this deal before someone else puts in an offer that gets accepted before we do." It wasn't that the deal was bad. I think he was in a rush and got some bad advice from someone who just wanted their commission. Over time, I'm sure it will be a great property.

What are your short-term and long-term outlooks? Are you a speculator? How do view your investments? Are you slowly buying properties that have lots of equity and great cash flow—or are you rushing in and making investments that might not be so great because you fell in love with the idea of ownership instead of the deal without thinking about how it will all play out. The first deals will be the catalyst for other deals down the road. Making the correct choices in the beginning should help build equity faster—and you will be able to continue investing with more momentum behind you.

We take a much different and much more aggressive approach then my friend did. We look for properties with lots of equity and appreciation with minimal fix-up costs. About the same time he bought his fourplex, we found a similar bank-owned building. The asking price was $155,000. Using our equity from other properties, we put together an all-cash offer. We knew it was a spectacular deal, and we bid it up an extra $30,000 over the asking price. We wanted the property and figured that would seal the deal. It did, and we ended up paying $179,450 after we deducted April's commission. I saw the history on the apartment, and it had sold for $280,000 ten years earlier. The deal was a true example of a diamond in the rough. Our total fix-up costs were $14,000, and the rents were $2,600 per month.

One year later, the appraisal came in at $281,000, which left $87,550 of equity sitting in the property that we will use to do our next deal. We had a grand slam because we were patient, knew the market, and bought correctly. We saw a great price, great rents, minimal fix-up costs, and a large equity position—and we did not have to put down any of our own money to do the deal. Not having to come up with another 25% down payment was nice.

We used the equity lines of credit from two of our other properties to buy the unit, and we had a large chunk of equity in the property because we purchased correctly. The new loan also included the $14,000 of our fix-up costs, which was given right back to us. Once we had permanent financing in place, we paid off the lines and were able to start shopping for other great deals again. Diamonds in the rough are hard to find, but they are out there.

If you keep looking patiently, the deals will eventually show up. I've never heard of any treasure hunter finding a great treasure on their first day of hunting.

KEEP YOUR EMOTIONS AWAY FROM YOUR SAVINGS.

CHAPTER 6

STOCKPILE

He who buys what he does not need steals from himself.

—Swedish proverb

If you're not a natural-born saver, this chapter might change the way you look at saving. If I can't persuade you to save after this chapter, be prepared to do some deep digging to get to the root of what's holding you back from not being able to save your money.

Why do so many people have such a hard time trying to save money?

1. **People have a very hard time seeing that far into the future. They can only deal with one day at a time.**
2. **If you're young, you might think you have plenty of time to save. If you're too old, then who cares might be your attitude. Both of these positions can be wrong.**

According to a 2017 GoBankingRates survey, 57 percent of all Americans have less than $1,000 in their savings accounts. That's just about enough for one small crisis. I think the number one reason most people spend instead of saving is because they do not have any definite plans for their money. Your money has no future. Your money has no mission. You have no goals to save for. With no goals, you have no reason to save just for saving's sake. Savings should be for investments and emergencies only! Build the investment portfolio and then buy the toys. If you do this correctly you'll have plenty of cash coming in to freely buy whatever you want.

Most of us have grown up with parents who never sat us down and explained the importance of savings. If your parents never took the time, I would guess their parents never did either. It sounds like a multigenerational problem. I always found it hard to learn something if no one was willing to talk about it, never brought it up, or if the subject does not seem to be of much importance in your circle.

How can one of the single most important subjects that can lead to your freedom get so easily overlooked? I guess that can change right now. For the 1st generation rich, savings will be the top contributor to help you jump-start your journey toward building personal wealth and generational wealth that can benefit everyone.

As a kid, I had a metal container that was full of change. I added to the pot whenever I had some coins to throw in. My brother always seemed to spend every penny he made. Sure, he had a few nice toys through the years—and I got to use some of them—but they eventually ended up at one of our garage sales or Goodwill.

If I had something of value, why shouldn't I sell it to recoup some of its value? If I bought it for fifty dollars, I would play with it and sell it for twenty-five dollars a few years later. If it still had some value, I was going to try to recoup it. With today's technology, it's super easy to sell almost anything—and it does not cost you one penny to try.

Being a saver came naturally to me, and I never struggled in that area.

If you can't seem to be able to save anything, then brew yourself a double shot of espresso, find a quiet corner, and break down your monthly expenses to get a clear picture of where all your hard-earned money is flying off to.

Hard-earned money did not come easy. It was earned hour by hour, day by day, and it was probably spent in less than two seconds. Every dollar you earn will get you closer to your goals if you start by saving some of it—or most of it. The more you save, the faster you can achieve your financial goals. It all comes down to one thing: your savings. Stockpile, accumulate, store, and hoard all the cash you can get your hands on—and then stick it in your new investment account. Keep your hands off it until you're ready to invest it.

"Living paycheck to paycheck will give you ZERO options."

Most people spend their entire monthly income on living expenses and non-necessities, which leaves nothing for their savings. Acts like that are foolish. You're throwing away the very thing that will help you reach your goals. You are walking a fine line and don't even realize it if you're not able to save any of your hard-earned money.

Did anyone see where all my money went? It's easy to spend yourself away from your goals. Living paycheck to paycheck is a way of life for majority of American workers.

According to a Career Builders survey:

- **78 percent of US workers live paycheck to paycheck to make ends meet.**
- **Nearly one in ten workers making $1,000,000+ live paycheck to paycheck. (WHAT!)**
- **More than one in four workers do not set aside any savings each month.**
- **Nearly three in four workers say they are in debt today—more than half think they will always be.**
- **More than half of minimum wage workers say they must work more than one job to make ends meet.**

If you fall into any of these categories and feel hopeless and trapped, find out how you ended up in those circumstances. Most of the traps can be avoided. You start by finding the cause. Get in front of a mirror. That might give you a clue to the problem.

No one likes to admit they are wrong, ask for help, or say they are weak. Acknowledgment of your weaknesses and not shifting the blame when you get into tough situations is a good start. Every decision—from beginning to end—begins and ends with you. Try not to get caught up always being number one when playing the blame game. Own it and go on.

Planning and saving your hard-earned money will make it easier to accomplish your goals and allow you to be more potent when it comes time to buying investments.

Potent is having great power, influence, or effect.

H.B.D.Y.W.I.

How Bad Do You Want It?

PART II

YOUR GREATNESS IS SEARCHING FOR YOU

HOW BAD DO YOU WANT IT?

A business tycoon was talking to an army veteran friend of mine who wanted to get into investing—but he did not have a lot of money at the time.

The businessman said, "How bad do you want it? Your mind-set should be like this. You need to do whatever it takes to make it. Do whatever it takes—even if it means sleeping in your car to save cash. Then do it!"

I love this story! It might be a little bit extreme, but he makes a good point about doing whatever it takes to reach your goals. Don't let anything or anyone stop you. If you must scale down to save, then start scaling down immediately. Sell your possessions to save. Don't eat out again until you can pile up a large savings. If you want it badly, that's what it takes. You need to think about saving money in those terms.

Do whatever it takes. Be extreme. "No," "I can't," and "quit" are words that have no meaning to you. It's more like do or die! Act like you don't have any safety nets. The 1st generation rich usually don't have safety nets. No one will bail you out if you get into trouble. Use this as motivation and pay attention to your financial health. Your savings account will be the best gauge of that. When you see that investment account growing, that's the sign you're beginning to win.

If you're never been picked on for being frugal, then you're probably not saving that much. All my friends knew I was super frugal. They joked that all the items in my house had price tags on the back of them. Everything was always for sale. Everyone around you should pick up on what you're doing just from the way you **don't** spend this incredible tool called money.

REWARD YOURSELF

Remember to always treat yourself to something when you meet your goals. That's when you spend on a **want**. Do it in a celebratory way. Every time you go and buy an investment, celebrate. Every time April and I have a large chunk of cash saved, we go investment shopping. Once we buy the investment, we buy the toys, collect art, or go on a vacation. As time goes on, we seem to celebrate more often. More of our goals are met—and the savings just grows.

How bad do you want it? What can you sacrifice now that can be purchased down the road when you have plenty of cash to spend on anything you **want**?

CHILDHOOD DREAMS

When I was growing up, just about every single kid on my block had some sort of glossy poster of an exotic sports car on their wall. By visiting my friends' homes, you would get a sense of what their idea of cool was by seeing what type poster they bought. My brother had the blue Lamborghini Countach, and I owned the red Ferrari poster.

We all dreamed about the day in the future when we could buy one of these exotic machines. We all bought and collected the plastic snap-together model cars, and we had plenty of Hot Wheels to keep that childhood dream alive.

Late one night, I was checking out used high-end sports cars at an online car dealership. A thought popped into my mind. I always wanted one of these dream cars, and by looking at the prices, I could easily afford one of the foreign beauties. Then, thankfully, my conscience took over. *Mark, you worked your tail off only to buy a super expensive supercar? That will only tie up a large chunk of cash—and you might miss out on other investment opportunities. There will be a time and a place for the expensive toys, but now is not that time. Keep making investments that have an opportunity to go up in value. Most likely, the sports car will go down in value. I guess I should shelve that want for the future. Expensive toys all have their time and place.*

Monkey see, monkey do is an expression to describe someone who imitates another person's actions—good or bad.

Once you have a good job and are making some extra money, you start saving like crazy. Your new savings account begins to build up. Then your best friend shows up at your house driving a brand-new sports car, and he's super pumped about his purchase. He says, "Let's take it for a spin!" He throws you the keys, and you jump in. The smell of the new leather hits your nostrils, you hit the accelerator like a NASCAR wannabe, and you fly down the street.

The euphoric feeling you get is out of this world. Your buddy starts telling you how incredibly easy it was to purchase the car.

Then you think, *Hmm! Maybe I could also buy a new car.* You just trade in your older high-mileage, paid-for vehicle for a brand-new right-off-the-showroom-floor; it's that easy.

WAKE UP!

That will keep you locked into high payments for the next five to seven years. Even if you have no problem affording the payment, you still missed the point. You need to have all your extra money working for you and not the other way around. Stay focused like a hungry lion and keep your eyes on the prey. If the lion does not eat, it starves. This gives the lion a good incentive to win at all costs.

This example goes for everything in our consumer-driven life. Am I saying that you should not buy new or expensive things? Do I come across like a penny-pinching, cheap, frugal guy who wants to take the fun out of buying anything? Maybe—but try to look at it from this angle. If done correctly, you will be able to buy just about anything you **want**. Buying a new vehicle at the wrong time might set you back years and many missed opportunities.

Keep your emotions away from your savings.

You set realistic, attainable goals, and then you make a detailed plan to reach your goals by doing whatever it takes to see your vision completed. Once you reach your first goal, it will build your confidence to make and reach for even greater goals in the future. Show yourself you can do it—and when you do, just repeat it.

Don't let anything creep into your path, especially new vehicles before you're ready. You might even justify it by thinking you deserve it—or you could die tomorrow so live every day like it's your last. Not true. Tomorrow will come—and you will most likely not die. That type of justification will utterly knock you out of trying to become 1st generation rich. It takes no effort to be just like everyone else by buying expensive toys and having tons of bad debt and no savings. Think what your savings can do for your future.

According to Northwestern Mutual's 2018 Planning and Progress study, the average American has about $38,000 in personal debt, excluding home mortgages.

> **"Learn to impress yourself, that's where greatness resides."**

IT'S HARD TO DO ANYTHING PRODUCTIVE IF YOUR HANDS ARE TIED.

This is just one example of the different financial challenges you will face on any given day. Replace car with any type of consumer item: diamonds, designer brands, vacations, or a million other unnecessary purchases that could keep you on the financial Ferris wheel: highs when you buy something and lows from being bored with what you just purchased. Get off the Ferris wheel of impulsive emotional spending.

Just because you can doesn't mean you should. Try to focus on just buying what you need, and over time, you will have plenty of cash to buy whatever you **want**. Remind yourself what your goals are and ask yourself if this purchase will bring you closer to your goals or make you more distant from them.

> **According to Wikipedia, deferred gratification is the ability to resist the temptation of an immediate reward and wait for a later reward. Deferred gratification is associated with resisting**

a smaller but more immediate reward in order to receive a larger or more enduring reward later.

Start today, choose correctly and don't let your future down.

The 1st generation rich must start somewhere, and savings is the best place to start. From your savings, you move into investing. The money from investing will give you the capital to reinvest and find more moneymaking investments. It is very difficult to invest without any money. This sentence sounds obvious, but so many people have such a hard time saving their money. Go fund yourself first and then buy your investments and then the toys—in that order.

The very definition of investing sums it up.

Investing is putting money to use, by purchase or expenditure, in something offering potential profitable returns, as interest, income, or appreciation in value.

Your savings is the main ingredient for building wealth. Once you have a pile of cash in your savings, it's time to start looking for investments. The investments you're looking for should pay you back every month so you will be able to rebuild your savings. You will be able to make more investments and continue the wealth cycle.

Imagine having an ATM machine in your garage. Once a month, an armored vehicle pulls up, and two armed guards cautiously walk toward your home with a bag of cash. One stands guard while the other guard fills it up. Each month, the same two guys fill your cash machine. If you're making the right investments, the bags get bigger and heavier. That's exactly what happens when you have a profitable business or large income that funds your cash-flowing investments.

Investments that make you money each month—even when you're sleeping.

PAY ATTENTION!

You work for one reason: so you have money to live and spend. You spend it on your needs: food, shelter, and other necessities. The normal response to any leftover cash is to buy your wants or whatever you want. Then, like that, your money disappears.

To build wealth that lasts, you need to find extra money after the necessities. If there is not much money that can be saved, be patient. You're going to make more as you work harder and find different ways to bring in more money. This is the beginning. This is your ticket to becoming 1st generation rich.

Work, spend on necessities, and save the rest. Build up your new savings account until you find an investment that fits you. The investment needs to pay you back to rebuild your savings so you can go shopping for more investments. This fascinating cycle continues, and the goal is to have options for numerous investments that continually rebuild your savings. The by-product of this is creating true freedom. Start small—and don't stop! Your future depends on you. Don't let it down. You have the potential. All you need to do is build a bond with patience. Everything takes time, but it's up to you to make it happen. How badly do you want it?

Nothing feels better than knowing your investments are paying for your mortgage, your vehicles, and all your other necessities each and every month. It all starts with having the discipline to save!

MRS. FORDA MOE MINT

Mrs. Forda Moe Mint grew up in a small family in New Mexico. She grew up in a small three-bedroom house with her little brother and a dog named Pilsner. Her mom was a stay-at-home mom who took great pride in keeping everybody happy in a clean and organized household. She always tried new recipes because she found it a joy to give her family new eating experiences. Forda's dad worked as a manager for a local radio station. His salary was just enough to pay all the bills and meet the family's needs. Her parents lived very conservatively. Their house was almost paid off, and her parents drove the same vehicles for twenty years.

Like most families, Forda's family never talked about money. Her mom would say, "It is what it is." Her dad worked hard, they ate good food, and they lived well. That was it.

It was almost evil to bring up the subject of money around the house. It made her parents feel uncomfortable. Forda's dad did not want to burden his kids when it came to the subject of money, and he would never talk about his income or finances.

Forda would occasionally ask her mom for money to buy this or to do that. "Can we go on a ski trip? Can we fly on our next vacation instead of driving? What about buying nicer clothes like my friends are wearing?"

The answer was always the same: "That's not in the budget. We don't have the money for those types of things."

Forda knew things were going to be a lot different when she grew up. She graduated from college with a student loan balance that was equivalent to the purchase price of a small house. That didn't matter she knew it would be paid off one day.

She ended up going to work for a startup advertising agency in sunny California. She worked incredibly hard like her dad and began to earn a great income. She could afford whatever her little heart wanted—and she did just that.

As soon as the money came in, she rented a pricey apartment full of custom Danish furniture in a sought-after neighborhood. She leased a Lexus convertible. She thought, *That's what everyone does when you make the kind of money I do.* Her weekends were all about shopping. Being so conveniently close to Beverly Hills helped her add multiple zeros to her maxed-out credit cards. She lived, looked, and acted like a true California millionaire. That never seemed to stop Forda Moe Mint because she lived for the moment. She thought, *I work hard. I deserve what I have. I could die tomorrow—so why not live for the moment?* Little did she know her motto was soon going to be her financial death sentence.

The party won't last forever, and then the bills come due.

Forda went to work one Monday morning and saw some empty cubicles. Her boss was walking around with a sad expression on this face. He asked her to come into his office. After they sat down, he looked at her with tears in his eyes and explained how they were having major financial issues because they lost one of their largest accounts and that a quarter of the staff would have to be laid off.

This sent a numbing chillness down her spine, which was followed by fear and anxiety. She walked away as beads of sweat began to form on her forehead. She slowly gathered up her belongings and walked out to her shiny Lexus. She was in complete shock. On the drive home, she thought, *How will I be able to pay for everything?* She lived paycheck to paycheck and had no savings. All her credit cards were maxed out, and she had no one to help her. All the sleepless nights that followed were beginning to make Forda sick. She was in a constant panic about not being able to sustain her posh lifestyle, which she thought she deserved.

On a long, sleepless night, she thought back to her childhood and how her parents lived. They did not seem to have much stress, and they were always able to live within their means. Forda, on the other hand, wanted everything now. She was young and was not thinking about her future. She thought she deserved to be happy—and living for the moment was supposed to bring that happiness.

She ended up landing a new job two weeks before her Lexus was going to be repossessed. Her new job paid about a third less than her old job did.

It was time to scale back. She stopped pretending to be rich. She decided to get rid of the Lexus and bought a used vehicle with low miles that an elderly couple was selling on Craigslist. She decided not to care what people thought about her. She began to feel more comfortable in her own skin. She stopped the daily shopping, and when her lease was up, she moved into a smaller, much more affordable apartment in a less desirable part of town. She wanted to buy a condo in the next couple of years because she decided to have a plan. With the money she was saving on rent, she worked at paying off her credit cards one by one until all the balances were finally paid off. Then the light bulb went on. She realized that if she had enough savings, she could weather any financial storm that came her way.

Forda's story might resemble a lot of people's current situations: living for the moment and not thinking about the future. If her parents had the tools and had taken the time to talk with her about the importance of savings and staying out of bad debt, her story could have been a lot different. She would have had many more years of making great financial decisions, which could have helped her build wealth instead of blowing all her income on things that did not matter. From the outside looking in, Forda seemed rich and successful. She had the best of everything, but she was one paycheck away from losing everything.

Money might be able to buy you a certain piece of mind—and it can make you more comfortable—but never depend on money to bring you any type of lasting happiness. The dessert is the prize for eating the vegetables.

I deserve it, and I can afford it. So why not?

Buying anything before you have the cash to justify the purchase is putting your money before your investments. Buying anything before you have real finances is poor reasoning. The dessert is the reward for eating the items on the plate that you're not that excited about. We forget this as we get older. Stay focused, and if you have to, just hold your nose. When you do it correctly, the reward will be waiting for you.

Don't justify away all your money just because you can and it's your right.

(__________) "not fully developed or grown acting in a childish way: having or showing a lack of emotional maturity." What word do you think fills in the blank?

THINK ABOUT IT

What's so great about money? What do most people think about when it comes to their money? Money has only brought problems to my life. Money equals anxiety. Money gave me all my worries and problems in the first place. Stress, stress, and more stress. I don't have enough money. I wish I had more of it. Money is the greatest problem-solver. Money must bring happiness. I work hard—why should they have nicer things than I do? Is money evil? How come I don't know any rich people or have any wealthy friends? I've never really thought that much about money. I have all the time in the world to make money. It seems like everyone around me is making it just fine. Money is taboo. I'm uncomfortable talking about it. Money was not brought up in my family discussions. How else am I going to learn about it? One day, I'll have to think about money, but until then, I really don't care. I'm way too busy to take the time to really look at my personal finances. I'm young I have all the time in the world. All I need is just enough money to get by today. I truly hope that I'll have enough money to retire and live comfortably. If that doesn't work out, I'm sure someone out there will hire me. My friends and family will certainly take care of me one day; they are my safety net, my retirement plan.

This has nothing to do with the love of money; it is about the function of it. Money is freedom. Freedom mixed with choices will give you plenty of options. Money is powerful. It motivates us, it moves us, and it feeds us.

Respected money is a powerful tool that can help educate us, and it can turn a bad situation into a better one. Money equals good health care options. Money invested wisely multiplies, which makes it easier to help others.

This is possible because you have plenty of extra money. You, your family, your friends, and strangers can all benefit from this little piece of paper. Money helps take some of the worry out of the equation.

Tools in the toolbox are useless unless someone picks them up and starts using them. Money is the same way. Money in a stack might make you feel rich. I always thought being rich sounded much better than just feeling rich or trying to be fake rich. As you respect money it can bring joy to you and others around you. Learn how to benefit from the proper uses that money can provide. Money can be your partner. The faster you learn this, the more time you will have to master it.

Paycheck to Paycheck = ZERO OPTIONS

CHAPTER 7

WHAT ARE YOU REALLY CALLED TO DO?

As you travel through life, the only regret you should have is that you didn't start this journey earlier.

This chapter is directed toward those who have no idea what they are meant to do. They never had the grades to be accepted to college. Or just decided that college wasn't for them. They are stuck in dead-end jobs, unhappy and unchallenged. They might be working for a boss who was doing your job three months earlier—and management thinks they miraculously have what it takes to lead.

There are a few options out there that you might be able to relate to.

OPTION 1

You're the boss. You worked hard to build and manage your business and investments. You take vacations with friends and family on your terms. You're in control of your own future. You decide you want to make more money this year, look at your costs, make a few adjustments, and fatten up your bottom line by bringing in some extra income or trimming some of the expenses.

By being your own boss, you give yourself more options. More options bring more freedom. Having options will always make tough decisions a lot simpler. Options give you more choices, which buys you the freedom to choose what you want or what's best for you. If you build the business, you get to make the rules. You're in control. It's your game, and you get to choose who you want to play it with.

OPTION 2

Some people can relate to this. You graduate from high school and choose a career you might be interested in. You choose something you think you might want to do the rest of your life. You work hard four to eight years, occasionally changing your major with the end goal of a diploma and a load of student loan debt to go with it. You look for a job that you hope will still be relevant in the next ten years. You settle into the culture you picked, and if you're highly motivated, you might decide to climb the corporate ladder all the way to the top.

You might have to deal with new bosses, corporate buyouts, layoffs, and transfers until you can finally retire.

The second option works for some people. They enjoy their jobs and the people they work with. If you find yourself on a career path you enjoy, you're one of the lucky ones.

Some fall into option 2 because no one showed them that option 1 was possible. If you never had close contact with a business owner, it might be hard to see yourself being one. Fear of failure will also keep you leaning toward option 2. The illusion of job security might also steer you toward option 2.

If you pick option 2, there's a good chance you will not be in total control of your future. Someone else might be making decisions on your behalf.

If you choose option 2 and settle in, you will have no idea what could have been. You won't know what having true options is really about. Your busy building someone else's dream. The world will have missed out on your great ideas. Your ideas might have changed everything, but you were unable to see that there was another path. You were not taught to look for the other path.

Option 1 does not discriminate against anyone. It welcomes newcomers into the world of entrepreneurship. It rewards those who diligently look for it.

My dad had a good job, a company car, good benefits, and an income to give us all a good life, but he had few options when it came to making decisions. I never heard him complain. He worked at the same job for twenty-five years, and that worked for my parents. They fell into option 2.

On the other side, I saw that having options was going to be our road to freedom. We chose option 1. We started to see similarities and patterns among other 1st generation rich business owners. Some of them had college degrees, but none of them were using them when it came to the businesses they started. Some never went to college or trade schools, but they became great investors. Some took a while to find their niche, and others found it right away. The most common thread we all had was the ability to stick to something that had the potential to become relevant in the marketplace.

Never accept mediocrity as being great. Never settle for just ok. Being comfortable should be reserved for retirement.

Have an idea, test it, and if it takes root, then grow it.

ANOTHER APPROACH

Travel another route. Find a franchise or a business for sale and start there. If it's a good fit and the numbers work, do the deal. Take the time to study and learn about what you're getting into. Take the company's financials to a good accountant. Make sure the numbers are correct.

We looked at buying an established business, and when our accountant checked out the numbers, we sometimes passed on it or were not comfortable after meeting the owner. Other businesses we bought and did owner financing for a year—and it worked out great. There are lots of ways to structure these deals. When it's time to get serious, find a professional you're completely comfortable with. Do not cut corners. Spend the money to see if the deal is clean before you negotiate.

A few friends bought businesses that did not work out. One of them hung in there and made it come together, and he has a booming electric business. My other friend had to sell his business at a loss. They both got into bad deals with the wrong people. They did not do their due diligence to dig into what they were really buying.

OBSERVATION

As time went on, I saw the freedom that Cool had. I figured I needed to make the best choice according to what I could see myself doing. I have never heard a self-employed business owner say they hated their work or the people they work with. Self-employed people have the option to pick who they want to be around. Most employees work for many different bosses and is stuck with unhappy people who also have little to no options. This is a combination for a toxic working environment. I could not see myself working nine to five to get a paycheck if I was not happy about what I was doing—with people I did not want to be around.

Self-employed people have the options to create great environments where their employees and contractors want to work at. If they end up getting a bad apple, they are removed immediately. They do have difficulties and problems, but they find a way to work through them.

When I meet with other 1st generation rich, we love talking about the paths that brought us to where we are today. We don't brag about how easy it was. We all probably work longer and harder than anyone else. In the end, the benefits outweigh the work—and it's well worth it.

PICK AND STICK

Pick something you like and stick with it until you begin to get some traction. When we started our business, it took a while to find the correct niche for what we were trying to do. We started as a residential delivery service and found a larger market for our business with commercial clients. We built the business by providing reliable service and competitive pricing. We stuck to it and watched it grow.

"You were placed on this earth to succeed. The only thing that can get in the way of that success is you."

If you picked something that did not work out, pick again. Keep going, keep moving, and never give up. I remember thinking, *If we just have seven deliveries today, all my expenses will be paid.* I sometimes spent hours hanging out in a public park just waiting for my phone to ring. I used that time to plan and dream.

We picked something and stuck to it. That was the key. We kept at it until it worked.

Your uniqueness is what separates you from the other

7,664,448,590

CHAPTER 8

ONE OUT OF BILLIONS

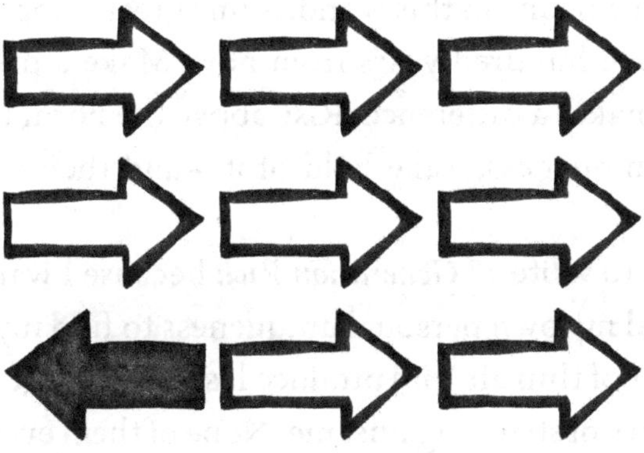

In 2018, the population of the earth was 7,664,448,590—and it is growing daily.

You're very unique. Why is there only one of you? Did you ever wonder why—out of the billions of people living on this beautiful planet—there is only one of you? Even identical twins who share the same DNA have their own unique qualities and differences, especially when it comes to their personalities. No one will ever look like you, talk like you, or have your same nature. You're truly one of a kind. No one has the same thoughts or emotions as you. Imagine if we did. I found a good word that describes that (boring.)

Find your uniqueness. Life is way too short to try to live someone else's biography. Create your own story. Make it come alive with your own dreams. Build something that benefits others. Try not to settle and just fit in by going about your daily life just like everyone else does. Recognize what makes you so unique—and then take the time to share it with others.

> **"Being the absolute best is great—it means you're #1—but being unique is greater because you're the only one."**

You are one of one in this world. Some great thing you do today may be felt one hundred years from now. Make a plan to be that person who makes a difference. Rise above the norm to claim your God-given uniqueness. Take hold of it—and then do something great with it.

I decided to write *1st Generation Rich* because I wanted to share the way I used my own personal uniqueness to find my path, create a business out of thin air, and produce lasting wealth by investing.

I had plenty of strikes against me. None of them ever stopped me or got in the way of any of my accomplishments. I never concentrated on my weaknesses, and I always leaned toward my strengths. I always thought I could pay someone to fill in the gaps in all the areas I was lacking. I never just sat there and waited for good things to happen to me. I'm sure I would have still been waiting if that were the case. Instead, I got up and decided to make something happen to me.

"Stop trying to be unique. You already are."

Your uniqueness is just waiting for you to make the first move. If you sit there, it will never show up. If you wait too long, you'll miss it. Take the time to explore and find out what makes you unique. Start to lay the foundation that your business can be built on. Your uniqueness is the cornerstone and starting point in this process. That is where your ideas will launch from.

Some people will find their uniqueness right away, and others will need time to search for it. Don't quit if you're having trouble pinpointing it. Your attitude should be slow and steady with complete focus. Keep exploring—and you will find it. Quitting is not going to be one of your options. Don't even entertain that idea.

EASY

Anyone can fill out a resume, walk into a business, and have a great chance of working for that particular company. Like everything, it's great until an unhappy boss or coworker rubs you the wrong way. Or you just don't find your work satisfying. You begin to dread every Monday morning. What do you do then? Quit? Do you stay there just because you need the money?

I would rather be in control my own choices than have choices made for me.

Change waits for you to make the first move.
Change is not pushy it's patient.

Dig into your uniqueness. Find out what's so special about you. What makes you want to get up in the morning? When you get up, are you excited about what the day might bring? If you're dreading what you're doing and can hardly stand your job—but you decide to stay anyway—then good luck. Everyone has that choice. It's called free will. Never accept mediocrity as being great. Never settle for something just because it's easy. Easy is what keeps you feeling comfortable—and then you're trapped.

Try shifting your thinking from an employee mind-set to one of a business owner. Start something that puts you in control of your own future. Give yourself a purpose when it comes to how you're going make your income.

VETERINARIAN BY CHOICE—OWNER BY ACCIDENT

A friend's wife was infatuated with animals. She studied hard to become a veterinarian. Once she graduated, she went to work for a local animal clinic. She immediately fell in love with her job, and she naturally connected with all her clients and their pets.

Due to the constant negativity of the owners, the morale inside the clinic was very low. Her husband saw how disappointed she was just about every evening when she got off work.

They decided to give it a shot and try to open their own clinic—and that is exactly what they did. They have a very popular veterinary clinic that has grown extremely fast because of their great service and friendly atmosphere. All of this became a reality because of a toxic working environment that she did not want to be a part of. She knew she could create something better on her own. She would not let anyone step on her uniqueness.

They created many more options for themselves, which never would have happened if she decided to stay at the other clinic. They were unintentionally thrown an opportunity, and they both saw it. They would have never thought such a bad atmosphere was just what they needed to realize they could do much better. Great ideas can come out of bad situations if you're looking.

WORK JAIL

You determine the length of your sentence.

CHAPTER 9

J. O. B.

Just Obey your Boss

Urban Dictionary defines a job as "at least 30 percent of your life is stolen from you to enrich the owners of a company making useless junk that some other poor person in a job will buy."

WORK JAIL

Your sentence starts the day you realize you have no passion for the work you're doing. One day, you wake up and realize you spent a large chunk of your life unhappy, bored, and grinding away doing something you couldn't care less about. Why settle for a job you're not happy with just so you can pay the bills and do it again next week and the following week after that?

You never really have the feeling of being in control of your future or being able to discover your real talents. You are working because you're stuck and feel you have no choices. You are counting the minutes until you're off—and the years until retirement. You are hoping everything will go as planned. This is the only type of jail where you get to choose the length of your sentence. You have the keys and can leave the facility any time you want to. It's your choice.

Once you're free, go find the path that most people will miss. When you find that path, it leads to true freedom.

> **Regret is a feeling of sadness, repentance, or disappointment over something that has happened or been done, especially a loss or missed opportunity.**

"No regrets" should be part of your vocabulary. Having no regrets is satisfying. Knowing you at least tried, gave it a shot, or just give it your best shot will release you from having any regrets in your life. You will never look back and say, "I should have," "I didn't," or "What kept me from trying?" Trying and failing is greater than never trying at all. Keep going—and the light bulb will go on.

"If you settle for the wrong career, you're voluntarily serving a life sentence in the prison of your choice."

You spend about a third of your life working. Business Insider says 87 percent of Americans have no passion for their jobs, and 80 percent of US workers are outright dissatisfied with their jobs. Most working-class people feel like they don't have much of a choice. They were taught to go to college and then hunt for a job. It might not be the dream job you were looking for, but it's a job. You get to work there until you get laid off, you quit, or retire. The masses fall into this category because that's what they were taught

That type of thinking will only help you build the jail you're going to spend the next twenty or twenty-five years working in. Work on building your freedom instead of being trapped in a place that will never let you discover your true potential. Never accept mediocrity as being great.

Many people who are ready to retire are hoping their retirement income will be able to cover all their living expenses. In 2017, 25% of Americans said they'll never be able to retire.

Misconceptions are views or opinion that are incorrect because they are based on faulty thinking or understanding.

Don't buy into misconceptions about not having choices. Everyone has choices. You choose to stay at a job you dislike. You choose to buy expensive clothes and cars before you have the money. You choose to spend all your income on things that will only give you a buzz for a moment and then do it all over again with your next paycheck.

You're the one who decided to run up your credit card each month and only pay the minimum balance. You decided to just wander through your working days without paying any attention or giving any thought to your retirement. You get to create your situation by your rash choices.

Your future is depending on you. Don't disappoint it.

If you make the right choices now, you will win. If you keep making the wrong choices, you will lose badly. You might not always be in control of your circumstances, but you're the master of your choices. By making the correct choices now, you are be setting yourself up for a future that is full of options. Who knows where you will end up? Give yourself the best chance possible to get there on your terms. You have the get out of jail free card. When are you going to use it?

Good choices over time will change your circumstances. Circumstances breed opportunities if you're paying close attention.

Options give you the power or right to choose.

SUNDAY NIGHT BLUES

Do you ever have those dreadful feelings on Sunday night, knowing that Monday is right around the corner? It is going to be another five full days of work or school. The hours slowly pass you by just like when you're waiting for your three-digit number to be called at your local pathetic government-operated Motor Vehicle Division. I had that same dreadful feeling every Sunday night. Just the word Monday made me feel depressed at times.

That feeling was gone when I genuinely enjoyed what I was doing. Imagine on Sunday night being just as excited to work as if it was Friday. That's the feeling we get now. Every day is a new experience full of new opportunities that are waiting to be noticed. We look forward to every day we can better our lives—and the lives of others. We are working toward goals that produce true freedom. Having options is what created the realization of Mondays feeling more like Fridays.

It's not all sunshine and roses every day. That would be a lie. We have great days and bad days around here. The rewards from reaching your goals and making it happen will be worth all the hard work no matter what type of day your having.

IT ALL STARTS WITH GOALS

This always brings me back to one thing. You must write down your goals on something permanent. Burn your goals into your mind. Tattoo them on your forearm. Make them a part of your daily life. Keep absorbing what you learned. Put it into practice. Reaching your goals and your new savings account is a great gauge of your progression. Pay attention, keep going forward, do whatever it takes, and never give up.

Options give you freedom. Having money is great, but having options is much better.

A Gallup study on the American workplace says two-thirds of us are disengaged at work. Of 100 million full-time employees, 51% are not engaged at work. They do the bare minimum and go through the motions to get a paycheck. They go in on Monday and work from eight to five doing the same thing every day until Friday comes around. The weekends are used for catching up on all the chores around the home that they were not able to finish during the week due to fatigue or exhaustion. That barely gives you any time to do the things you really enjoy doing.

Freedom is "the power or right to act, speak, or think as one wants without hindrance or restraint."

True freedom has no boundaries. Nothing is holding you back except yourself. Freedom is doing what you want to do when you want to do it and doing it with whoever you want. That sounds like a little kid throwing a fit, but it's the truth. Total freedom is having no boundaries and having many options to choose from.

BUYING TIME

When we started to see our plans coming together, I felt we needed more time to focus on the business and the investing side of things. Having a spotless home was a must for us, but spending the time to clean it was not. Hiring a housekeeper to clean once a week bought us some much-needed extra time. Suddenly, we had one less thing to deal with and an extra five hours per week to spend how we wanted to. More options equals more choices.

With more options, we were able to examine our life and see if an area needed improvement. We are now able to sub out all types of time-consuming labor and spend more time with family, friends, and investment hunting. We can plan extended vacations if we want to. If I get the urge, I can play eighteen holes of golf, mountain bike, hike, camp, paint, or relax and do nothing. We built a well-oiled moneymaking machine that essentially creates pockets of time in areas that used to steal our precious time.

> **You can have a high income with no options. What good is that? Having money is great, but having options is much better.**

Options were made by making the right choices over time. You cannot put a price on the freedom that comes from having options. I'm in control of my future and my family's future, and that's priceless. Doors will unlock in all sorts of areas because I have time to rest, think, and create our own opportunities.

REMEMBER

When we were kids, our minds were free and not full of distractions. We played and dreamed and just let our minds travel. Having time to relax lets our minds catch up and wonder. Some of my greatest ideas have come to me in those quiet moments. Give your mind time to think. Think about ways to create more options in your life; when the big decisions come knocking, you will be able to make them confidently because there will be less pressure involved. Buy yourself time to relax and think. Rash decisions could have lasting consequences.

REMEMBER THE SIT 'N SPIN?

The only person I know who made money from sitting and spinning was the inventor of the Sit 'n Spin. It's an absolute blast if you're under the age of ten—but not so much as an adult. The Sit 'n Spin can sum up some people's lives. It's the same thing day in and day out. It's a boring existence with limited opportunities or a high-pressure working environment with a cranky boss.

No one goes to an interview thinking they are going to be miserable after a few months on the job. So why does it happen? What makes humans settle for something that brings them no joy, no sense of accomplishment, and no satisfaction just to get a paycheck every two weeks. After a while, you could become the person who is making the job difficult for others because you're not happy with your own situation. When you're not happy, everyone suffers.

The Sit 'n Spin is settling for what's in front of you. Your motto is "It could always be worse. Someone has to do this job. It might as well be me."

ADVANTAGES OF THE ENTREPRENEURSHIP

Entrepreneurs might have a greater chance of making a larger income, which would equate to more money to save and invest. Most employees get the same paycheck every two weeks. Most of the checks get eaten up on simple living expenses that always seem to go up, which doesn't leave much to put into their savings accounts. Also, employees pay the most when it comes to taxes. They have few or no tax deductions. Business owners and investors get the best tax breaks, which will help put cash right back into your savings. More savings equals more investments to go shopping for.

CHANGE?

Change is to give a different position, course, or direction to. To make a shift from one to another.

Is it possible to transition from a dead-end job to one you love? What would make someone leave a job that has a sense of security to venture into the unknown and give up what might look like certainty for something that may seem uncertain? If you're feeling too much fear, doubt, or worry—or you just have cold feet and think you could never make that change—it's completely up to you. Stay where you are—and another year will go by if you change or don't change. If you want it badly enough, you'll find a way to do it.

Doesn't society need large numbers of people working different jobs to keep humanity—or your part of the world—running smoothly? Exactly. If it wasn't for all those types of jobs, life would be quite different. Imagine having to haul away all your own decomposing trash in the back of your minivan every week. Good luck trying to locate the city landfill. Imagine having to spend the time cleaning up your hotel room when you're done using it.

We all love the conveniences society provides when it comes to certain jobs, and we should never take them for granted. We're super thankful that there are people out there who have no problem doing it. Some people are just happy to work a job that puts food on the table and pays the bills. You never hear those people complaining.

I'm not trying to throw large rocks at hornets' nests. Most people, by nature, don't like any type of change. Change feels unnatural. I'm speaking directly to the person who feels like it's time to start making some changes in life, try something outside of their current circumstances, step out of their comfort zone, and do something different, something new, and something that will breathe life into their day.

Imagine coming home every night tired but with a smile on your face. I'm sure everyone around you will enjoy that also. Imagine having a feeling of accomplishment instead of dread. It will begin to energize you instead of discouraging you. Most people don't realize they have access to those options. This journey starts when you pick a different path to freedom—one that is not clearly marked.

If you have always wondered or daydreamed what it would be like to work for yourself, be the boss. Build something amazing that everyone could benefit from. It could be passed down to other generations or be sold. You have that option. We all do! You have the same access to the path we traveled on. The one path that is overlooked and less traveled turned out to provide us with complete and total control of our time and income. That path provided the cash for multiple investments that pay us back every month. That was our main goal, and it worked.

1st Generation Rich is about showing you that anyone can make something great. With an idea— starting with no money, no safety nets, and very minimal education—we were able to find a very different path to success.

You will start your journey the day you decide there is more to life than just accepting mediocrity as being great. Think beyond what you were told, step outside the normal way of doing things, and tap into your greatness. Change is the first step.

Greatness comes when you realize you are great.

What does it take to get there? Rewire your thinking from that of an employee to that of a business owner. Everything we do as human beings has a beginning that originates in our heads. Thoughts go in, and some go back out. Try to translate your ideas into a goal—and then begin to lay out a blueprint for how to make that goal a reality.

My plan was simple: pick up from point A and deliver to point B.

Delivering great customer service, becoming the best at what we did, and repeating it over and over built a base of clients who trusted us with their fragile cargo. As time went on, we added divisions to the company. We grew steadily and profitably. That was the key to our get rich steady plan, and it worked.

NO SUCH THING AS CRAZY

I could never imagine that a biofuel company could produce oil from growing algae in the middle of the desert or a shrimp farmer could create a high-altitude ocean in the middle of a rural desert community. Everything starts in the mind and works its way to reality.

HOBBY TO BUSINESS TO PROFIT

I have a relative who loved creating embroidery designs. She had a demanding full-time job and was only able to do digitizing at night or on weekends when she could fit it in. She started creating her own custom designs, and after some time, she started building a large portfolio of logos and sayings. She knew her designs were unique, and no one was selling her patterns anywhere. She found a great website that catered directly to the embroidery industry. Her unique designs were a hit from day one, and they started selling immediately. She created a second stream of income out of thin air from something she loved to do, and she did it only being able to work when she found the time.

Having an income-producing business made retirement that much easier. Once she retired and had more time, she began to grow her business. It started with a hobby and turned into a business that will provide income until she stops or decides to sell it. She created options that will carry her into a comfortable and prosperous retirement.

Dreaming is easy; everyone should dream. It's the doing that takes the effort. Combining these two parts is the first step of your journey. Everything starts with an idea and moves to action. Most ideas never take off due to inaction. Inaction and distraction are the big dream killers. Be on guard against both. It's almost as if your mind looks for the easiest way to get something done. Effortless, low-energy shortcuts produce pennies instead of dollars.

Ideas turn into goals, goals turn into work, and work provides options, which creates freedom. Freedom naturally follows from what the options provide. This happens over time—not overnight. Be tenacious. Push forward at all costs. Don't settle for shortcuts. Work as if your future is depending on you.

This journey, if done correctly, will bring you to places and experiences you never thought were possible. Find out what you were made to do—and start making it happen to you.

CONVERSATION NON-STARTER

"Try not to work too hard." I hear that silly expression a lot when I'm working. That saying drives me nuts. Maybe it is supposed to be a conversation starter. I never hear any business owners saying it.

If you think anything in this book can be done without working hard and smart, then you missed the whole point. Anyone can go and get a job you might be bored with in six months to a year.

> **Hard work makes everything happen. Never settle for an easy job—or you might be the one telling the customers to try not to work too hard.**

Try to work smarter and harder, dream big, and create your own path to wealth. Don't depend on anyone else for your success. Work like you don't have a safety net to catch you if you fall. It's do or die. It's easy to fill out an application, and I filled out plenty before I started my business. Most of us start out that way. The goal is to be the one looking at all the applications and not filling one out.

This venture is completely and entirely in your hands. You hold the only keys to unlock your success. The process of starting a business and investing will fall on your shoulders in the beginning, and the decisions you're making will steadily bring you to the finish line (**freedom**). It's a get rich steady attitude. Wealth will come when you build on a solid foundation. It happens one small dollar at time. One small dollar saved next to other dollars will someday be put to work multiplying and growing as you build your own personal cash machine.

YOU

Find out how you tick—and then explore other avenues to get you to where you want to go. Starting is the hardest part. If you have the right idea at the right time and an attitude of not accepting failure at any cost, you have what it takes to go and make it happen.

Just get started!

MOTIVATION

+

FOCUS

+

REPETITION

=

GREATNESS

PART III

THE MAGIC BEHIND THE MAGIC

MAGIC

When a good magician shows you a great magic trick, it can blow your mind and make you seriously question your own reality. Magic works because the trick makes you think it was impossible. The magician might even break the code of secrecy and show you how the illusion was created. Once you see how easy and simple the trick was, it's hard to believe you were so easily fooled.

Building a business and buying real estate might look complicated and unattainable from the outside. However, when you learn the basic principles that are involved, the process becomes simplified. What might look impossible from the outside—like a magic trick—becomes attainable with the right ingredients.

Despise Distraction

"Distraction steals your attention and dilutes the focus that's needed to finish what you started."

CHAPTER 10

DISTRACTIONS

Choices + goals + focus + time - distractions = options.

If trying to build wealth is that easy, how come everyone doesn't do it? The four main ingredients to accumulating wealth are creating an income, saving it, investing it, and repeating it. If you do all four things for long enough, you can retire wealthy.

It sounds so simple. How come everyone's not doing it? One of the main culprits is distraction, which prevents people from giving their full attention to something. Being obsessed with anything that interferes with your creative process will slowly pull you toward the extinction of your dreams. Distraction never helped anyone accomplish anything. It kills dreams, passion, and the ability to get anything done.

Distractions will own you. Distractions will gladly dictate how you're going to spend your precious time. One small, unnoticeable minute at a time, distraction steals something you can never get back.

"Focus finds all the materials needed to build success."

Our normal propensity as human beings is to be distracted. It doesn't take that much. You will never have to go looking for distractions; they will always come looking for you. Look at everyone around you. When I'm sitting in any public place, three-quarters of everyone around me is busy staring at their screens. No interaction at all. You have no idea how many opportunities your missing. That's just people in public. When they get home, the TV and a hundred other distractions own their attention. Don't be a slave to these devices. Have some restraint and balance. Distraction is the nail in your tire. It's the unseen termite inside your walls that is slowly eating away at your studs.

Your cell phone has a built-in app that keeps track of all your screen time. You might be surprised by how much time you're spending peeking into other people's lives. Other distractions have nothing to do with your cell phone or TV. There is always going to be something competing for your attention. Something will eventually sidetrack you from reaching your goals.

What is the conclusion when it comes to distractions? If you find yourself easily distracted and not able to concentrate clearly, your attention will not be focused on the task ahead. It's too easy to lose your drive and the reason you started this journey in the first place.

Don't let distractions become your dream killer. Distractions will keep you from reaching your full potential—if you let them. Guard your time with the attitude that every day on this earth counts toward your progression (not regression).

STAGNANT

Pay attention so you don't find yourself drifting toward stagnation. Picture a pond of stagnant water full of leaves, dead insects, and debris. The foul smells, the coating of green scum, and all kinds of bacteria reside in the soupy mixture. Water needs to be constantly **moving** in order to be safe and clean. Water needs to have an inlet and an outlet. Covet your time so it won't be wasted on mindless and nonproductive activities that will steal your focus and slowly draw you toward stagnation. Get rid of any contaminants that could creep into your daily routine and gently tease you off track. Over time, the littlest things can destroy your progress.

The tiny purchases can drain your bank account over time. Distracted drivers create most of the vehicle collisions we see. Pay attention and shun distraction daily. Be on guard against this enemy. It sneaks into your daily routine by stealing your focus and burning your goals.

Focus is the center of interest or activity.

Of course, there is a time and place for unproductive activities. Just make sure you're setting good boundaries when it comes to them. Put a short leash on the unproductive, mind-numbing, fruitless activities that will tug you away from success. It's a good idea to constantly check yourself. Conduct a personal audit on all the activities you're currently doing.

- **Is it bringing me closer to my goals?**
- **How am I impacting the people around me?**
- **What type of people am I associating with?**
- **Is my behavior improving my chances of success?**
- **How are the decisions I'm making now going to change what happens in the future? Every decision will have some sort of consequences down the road.**
- **If I happen to get off track, how will I recognize it? How do I reconnect with my original goals and dreams?**
- **What are my energy levels? Read chapter 12 if you feel like you don't have the energy to continue.**

Everyone will have unexpected setbacks that no one saw coming. You will certainly not be exempt from any problems. You will have high highs and low lows. How you handle these will set a precedent for dealing with the future problems that will surely come your way. You will always have a better chance of success if you stay focused and don't give up! Chip away until you reach your goals. Slow down only when you have accomplished what you set out to do. Only stop long enough to create even greater goals.

Throw your expectations in the trash. Expect that some things will go your way and some will not. Don't let your expectations take you off course. Stay in sync with your ideas and see them to completion. Make changes when necessary. Change is not always your enemy. It directs and opens your eyes into new areas that you might have not been able to see before.

> **Help makes it easier for someone to do something by offering one's services or resources.**

Don't be shy or embarrassed to ask for help. We all need some help from time to time.

Most of the 1st generation rich did not have anyone to help them get started or give them encouragement to keep going in difficult times. I never had a mentor to help me on my journey. I joined a weekly businessmen's group with 115 business owners. I was constantly gathering useful information at these meetings, always asked lots of questions, and realized that most businesses have a lot of the same issues. Everyone deals with the same problems. It was a relief to know that I wasn't the only one dealing with these issues. Everyone was dealing with the same basic stuff, but most of the guys had figured out great ways to solve their problems.

AMBITIOUS

I spent hours and hours reading, researching, and listening to podcasts. I soaked up any information I could get my hands or ears on. I was always watching biographies of successful businessmen I admired to build my self-confidence. I knew that what I was pursuing would be possible to accomplish one day.

Stay connected with people who are moving forward with their journeys. Associate with those who share the same attitude toward money and the uses of it. Be quick to move away from anyone who tries to squash your desire to become successful. Never listen to negative people who have never tried to step out of their own little comfort zones to better their lives. On the other hand, take full-page notes from successful people in areas you're interested in.

I believe everyone must find their own way. No matter what kind of help you're getting—or not getting—find a path that will end up breathing life into your daily work. That's the goal. That's the endgame. You'll have no regrets if you set goals, seek good counsel when needed, and focus on what will help you grow rather than cause you to become distracted. What you focus on, you will complete. Just get started.

NO TURNING BACK

On a sunny afternoon in August, a friend and I made plans to climb a trail to the top of the Sandia Mountains. Our goal was to summit the mountain before sunset. The mountain was 10,678 feet above sea level. My friend had tried climbing the trail a few weeks earlier but was not able to finish the climb. We decided to give it a shot together. In hindsight, I should have asked why he was not able to complete the climb the first time. I would shortly find out.

We started our adventure to the top of the crest at noon. At first, the climb was easy. The single-track trails were clearly marked. As we climbed, the trail faded away and started to show signs of extreme difficulties. We noticed fewer climbers on the trail, but it didn't stop us at all. We were eager to see what was ahead.

We worked our way up a large crumbled rock formation where we had to have three points of contact at all times in order to not fall off the trail. Many hours later, we saw a single-engine airplane flying right under us. That was when we realized how high we really were. We foolishly kept pushing forward until we came to a group of climbers who were all decked out in climbing gear with ropes and harnesses.

That's when we knew we were in some serious trouble. We

were unprepared amateurs on a technical climb. We ended up on the pinnacle of an extremely difficult rock spine that had a two thousand-foot sheer vertical drop on each side of this large boulder that we needed to get around. The path to the other side had a very tiny ledge that led to a couple massive builders we had to climb over.

We looked at each other and decided it was going to be way too dangerous to descend from that point. We began to slowly find our way around the rocks with some direction from the seasoned climbers who were probably wondering what the heck these two unprepared fools were doing. When we finally reached the other side, we were exhausted and excited. We agreed that our adventure was extremely intense and rewarding, but we had no plans to ever attempt that climb again.

We had set a feasible goal to summit Sandia Peak. We got to a point where it was safer to keep climbing than it was to turn around. We had to push through. We worked our butts off maneuvering around some of the roadblocks that stood in our way to ultimately make it to the top of the mountain. I learned more about myself and more about being pushed to my limits with fear, stupidity and faith in others than in any other experience I've ever had. I finally understood why there were so many mountain climbing analogies.

Mountains are hard to climb. They push us and move us outside of our comfort zones. Mountains have so many different paths to take. Some are easy, and some are challenging. Pushing yourself physically will also strengthen you mentally.

Try spending a day hiking or go to one of your favorite hangout places with a notepad and a cold drink. Be prepared to write or draw whatever you think your future should look like. Be as descriptive as possible. It doesn't matter what comes out of your pen—just let the pen do its job. Write and rewrite—and don't forget to date it. Dates are very important. You want to be able to look back and see your progress. I also write down where I was when I was writing.

Reflection brings back the same inspirations and feelings I had that day.

PEN IT

I started writing down all of my goals and wants once a year. I continually check them to see which ones were achieved and to make sure I am always staying on track. Every New Year's Eve, I add up my net worth, always making sure I am saving enough money for my future investments.

When it came time to harvest, we were ready financially and comfortable with the investments we had chosen. We transferred all our hard work (new savings) to the investments that pay us back each month.

Get rich steady. Plant, harvest, and repeat. Find your niche and make that niche your passion. Passion is what drives the creative side of us to flourish.

> **Passion is when you put more energy into something than is required to do it. It is more than enthusiasm or excitement.**

Passion is ambition that is materialized into action. Put as much heart, mind, body, and soul into something as is possible.

WATCH YOUR STEP!

Distracted, being unfocused, wandering, and having low energy are the four great dream killers. They prevent you from ever getting close to seeing what could have been. In a sense, these four blinders mask your true potential. Pay attention and recognize them as poison to your progress, goals, and dreams.

You won't find any hidden secrets to becoming a millionaire in this book. There are no secrets, no magic, and no tricks. Instead, it's all about positioning yourself in the marketplace to take advantage of the moneymaking investments that will come your way. Be ready with knowledge and finances to jump on the train as it passes. Set the groundwork for yourself to see all the opportunities that are constantly surrounding you. If the train passes you by, remember there is always another train right behind it. You will have multiple chances to ride the train when you decide it's time to use your ticket. Your ticket never expires.

Failure only comes to those who quit.

WHEN EVERYTHING IS JUST RIGHT

CHAPTER 11

THE GOLDILOCKS WINDOW

Endless opportunities are everywhere

The ages between thirteen and thirty-five are called the Goldilocks window. It's the years when everything is just right. That's the period when you're trying to figure everything out and thinking you will have all of eternity to do it. Your horizon is about to explode with your journey into the unknown. It feels like the world is your playground. Endless opportunities are everywhere. It's a great time to dream about what the future might look like.

You should have little to no debt and not too many responsibilities or boundaries. You can go anywhere. You can get involved with anything at any time. You have plenty of time to meet, greet, and eat with anyone. It's freedom at its finest.

Then you notice all your friends are picking schools to go to. Some of your friends know exactly what they want to do. They pick out a college and hope for a bright future. Most of my high school friends fell into that category. Some went on to get high-paying jobs in areas they loved. Others did not. We all had one thing in common. We all picked our own paths to travel.

You choose. Should you go to college or use the money to buy a franchise to run. Go to a trade school to learn a trade so that one day you can own your own business? Pick a major and get a degree and find a great job. Maybe your state offers lottery scholarships or grants to help you pay for your college tuition. You might be one of the lucky ones whose parents started a college fund and can go to the school of your choice.

The choices you make every day determine your future. The choices you make from here on out will shape the choices you need to make in the future. Some choices will be a horrible mistake and might slow you down or pull you off the track, and other choices will have the opposite effect by drawing you closer to your goals. Either way, there's nothing like being able to make your own decisions.

If you fall within the Goldilocks window, your chances of becoming rich will greatly increase due to time. You will have plenty of time for trial and error when starting something. You will have plenty of time to get it right. You will have plenty of time to start all over if you get it wrong. You will have plenty of time to try out different ideas.

When I was twenty, I said, "I'm going to take huge risks before

I'm thirty." It sounded great in theory, but I never really did it. I decided I would try the get rich steady plan. I felt this path had a better chance of success. I was always planting seeds, watering, tending, and harvesting the cash when the time was right. I was turning around and investing the cash into our business and then into investments. When everything was growing, I noticed I had much more time at my fingertips. Creating more time gave us the freedom to fine-tune our business and hunt for more investments.

"We all get the same amount of time each day, those who learn to respect it are the ones who prosper."

The Goldilocks window is all about time. Time is yours; you own it. It belongs to you, and then you begin to share it with others. If done correctly, you will have time and opportunities on your side. They will be working with you in your corner. If you choose to waste time, it will gladly let you. Harness your time to make a difference. Time is just as important as your money; if spent incorrectly, you'll have nothing to show for it.

If you are in the Goldilocks window, wake up and recognize that it is the greatest carefree period of time to find a passion a business and investing opportunities. Don't let this prime time in life pass you by. You don't want to be standing in the station never getting on the train. We all get the same amount of time, but those who learn to respect it are the ones who will end up prospering.

I DO

According to *Women's Health,* the average age of a first marriage in 2017 for women was 27.4 years, and for men, it was 29.5.

Things happen very quickly after marriages and kids. Time does not seem to be present. Having a plan before you dedicate yourself to these life experiences is one way to stay focused before the season changes.

It's never too late to start a company or build wealth. Of course, the earlier you start, the better. It's easier to take larger risks before you have a family and settle into a marriage. Some people feel as if time has passed them by or they missed the golden window of opportunity to start investing or build a business.

It's never too late to start investing; money doesn't discriminate against anyone. Money has no feelings. It doesn't care about who you are, what you look like, how old you are or how you handled it in the past. Money doesn't do background checks, but money is attracted to those who respect it and learn to manage it correctly. Money does have its favorites. It favors those who appreciates its true value. Never confuse the love of money with the function of it and it's never too late to start.

DEAD END OR NEW BEGINNING

No matter where you are right now, at this very moment in life, you can always transition into new challenges and life-changing opportunities. Opportunities are all around you—and they are just waiting for you to trip over them. You need to be constantly on the hunt, looking for your opportunities. Look at every business and investment you can get your eyes on. Also look in other states to get ideas about other thriving businesses that you might want to bring back to where you live.

COPYCAT

I met a small business owner who started an organic ice cream shop. She freezes the ice cream ingredients with liquid nitrogen right in front of you. Watching the process was amazing. They use these thick cryo gloves and face shields to protect against spills. All the ingredients were added in a large mixing bowl—and then comes the liquid nitrogen. A large white cloud fills the air, and within a few seconds, it's complete and ready to enjoy. It was this entertaining, and the ice cream was delicious.

When the owner and her husband were on vacation in California, they stumbled across a little ice cream place. The lines were stretched around the building. They tried it and loved it so much they decided to bring the concept to their hometown.

Opportunities are circumstances that make it possible to do something. Opportunities are all around you. They are just waiting for you to discover them.

A West African proverb says, "One who waits for chance may wait a year."

REMOVE THE BLINDERS

Pedro is a hardworking immigrant from Mexico who ended up working for a large landscaping company in town. He worked with them for thirteen years and decided to venture out on his own. He started out small with one other guy and took every job he could get his hands on. His motto was "If you need something done, I will find a way to do it." That was his ticket. His goal was to find a way to make it happen.

Every property and new home can use the skills of a good landscaper. Pedro saw this and knew he was a great landscaper. Pedro saw something that was right in front of everyone else he worked with, but he was the only one who went and grabbed it. He worked with eighty other guys, and they were all great at what they did. Pedro stepped up and found the path that the other eighty guys missed. He created a thriving business. He grabbed a large chunk of the wealth that was right in front of him. He took a chance, stepped out of his comfort zone, and became 1st generation rich.

You're in a good place if the only regret you have is that you didn't start your business sooner.

PRIME

If something is in its prime, it is at its best. The same goes for people. If you are young and healthy and in the prime of your life, you are ready to take on the world. That's a great time to start a business. When is it too late to try to make a change or begin a business? When your comfortable. When you decide to settle it's hard to be motivated.

Any one at any age can try. Success without passion is just dreaming.

It's always too late if you never try

Everyone buying real estate was making money before the Great Recession of 2009. Some of my friends were buying homes and selling them and making $50,000 profit within six months. Some of those same friends also lost some of their homes to foreclosure when the homes lost all their value. Timing is everything

BE ON THE LOOKOUT

Research, research, research. Make time to dig deep in an area that might interest you. Don't be discouraged if you don't find something right away. It might not happen overnight, so keep pushing forward until the light bulb in your head turns on.

Building a business and investing is going to be a process. It feels more like a marathon than a fifty-yard dash. Patience and endurance working in tandem are what is needed when you begin to step out and start exploring your ideas.

Ideas clear the way for other ideas to evolve.

A couple of my brother's friends were always driving around our neighborhood in different types of cars. I later found out that these guys were buying and flipping all these different types of muscle cars.

An idea popped into my head. If they could do it, maybe I could give it a shot. I started thinking about how I could get involved, and a few months later, I was flipping old Volkswagens because that's all I could afford at the time. The process was fun, and I was instantly hooked.

I was in the business of buying, restoring, and selling vehicles for about two years. I started hanging around with an old schoolmate.

Zach noticed that I was always working on broken-down cars in my driveway. He asked a lot of questions about what I was doing. He was excited, and I knew he was about to get bitten by the entrepreneurial bug. He said, "I wish I could start a business like you did."

We talked about doing a venture together. He was brainstorming with his family, and his mom suggested that we should start a courier service. At that moment, the seed was planted.

Because of my little car-flipping business, Zach brought another idea to my attention. I recognized another great opportunity. It turned out to be my main source of income for many years and funded all our other investments. One small step led to other opportunities that grew into many different opportunities over time. Every venture will have a process that works when combined with patience and endurance. Certain chains of events have a funny way of directing you to other unseen opportunities.

Once you create your own path and start seeing your opportunities, a funny thing starts to happen. Opportunities will turn in your favor and start moving toward you. They're much easier to spot. It's kind of like when you buy a car and then notice how many other people have the same great taste as you do. Their cars were always on the streets, but until you bought yours, you never really noticed them before.

Prepare yourself so you will have the best chance to find opportunities. Opportunity knocks, but if you don't answer, it goes elsewhere.

"Exercise will prevent your family from collecting their inheritance early."

CHAPTER 12

WHAT'S THE HEALTH?

You only get one of these priceless machines

Why do some people take better care of their cars than their bodies? They are waxing and washing every weekend, using the best-performance motor oil, filling up with premium gas, and treating their vehicles to spa treatments. All the while, they are neglecting something that has a much greater value.

At birth, you were given one, rare, unique machine. Your body is one out of seven billion. You grow, learn, develop, explore, and conquer all in this priceless machine. You only get one of these—so try not to blow it, misuse it, or abuse it. It does not come with any spare parts. You're stuck with it until the end.

Your health is by far the single most important factor for having the physical and mental energy to handle all the rolls, challenges, and hats that you're going to wear when starting out.

Say goodbye to the work hours of 8:00 a.m. to 5:00 p.m. In the beginning, you'll probably work longer hours. Your health will play a large factor in all aspects of your business.

"Exercise will give you the competitive edge needed to perform at your best."

We all sometimes fall into this trap. You stay up late and wake up early. Your idea of eating healthy is ordering extra lettuce and tomato on your Big Mac and washing it down with a small diet cola. You repeat the pattern every weekday until the weekend comes around again. By then, you're exhausted and sleep-deprived. What are the chances that your productivity over the weekend will be nonexistent? If you're tired, I get it. You had a long week, and your weekends are for playing not working.

You might have a long workweek in the beginning. When you start seeing success, you might try cutting back on the long hours.

Delegate your work to others with the goal of not having to work as much—unless you want to.

Everyone needs a good amount of rest. We were not made to go all the time. I personally try to take every Sunday off to recharge. I'm amazed how productive and rested I am for the following week.

GETTING THE EDGE

In every sport, athletes are always looking for a competitive edge. They want any little boost to help them be just slightly better than their competition. Being in top physical shape will give you the edge you need to win.

> **Urban Dictionary says exercise is "something you don't do because you spend too much time on the internet."**

Here are a couple of reminders about exercising and diet:

1. **You will greatly increase your chances of living longer. Isn't one of the main reasons you're trying to build wealth is so you can enjoy it as you age?**
2. **Exercising will give you more energy. Studies have proven that regular exercise increases your energy levels and reduces fatigue.**
3. **It helps you get better sleep.**
4. **It reduces stress and relieves anxiety.**
5. **It improves your memory.**
6. **It strengthens your immune system.**
7. **Mental energy is just as important as physical energy.**

Who doesn't like benefits, especially when they benefit you? The direct benefits that come from exercising make it clear that it needs to be a part of your weekly success plan. Build an exercise program that you will commit to. Hire a trainer at a gym. Read books, blogs, and fitness websites that interest you. Do something to get the stamina you need to win. It will always pay off.

When it comes to building your business and investing, you also need to give yourself a competitive edge. Your health will be a huge contributor to your success. When you're feeling great, you're at the top of your game. You feel invincible when you're eating good food and exercising regularly. Your problems or issues seem less important. Everything's not as big of a deal as it is when you're tired or exhausted. You just deal with it and go. Getting enough sleep, eating healthy, and exercising will contribute to your mental state. A strong mind, plenty of sleep, and a strong body will give you what you need to keep pressing forward.

Everyone is unique in how they function. Find out what works best for you—and then do it. This is an individual game when it comes to your health. It's not a group sport. Personalize an exercise program that is completely custom to fit you and your schedule. Stick to it because the benefits will outweigh the consequences of doing nothing.

GET RICH QUICK?

Gives False Hope

to the Lazy.

CHAPTER 13

NO PHISHING

Too good to be true

According to Wikipedia, phishing is the fraudulent attempt to obtain sensitive information such as usernames, passwords, and credit card details by disguising as a trustworthy entity in an electronic communication.

A Ponzi scheme is a form of fraud in which belief in the success of a nonexistent enterprise is fostered by the payment of quick returns to the first investors from money invested by later investors.

You're not going to believe this! I received an e -mail from a long-lost relative living overseas who said I just inherited $16 million. I've always wondered if people really fall for those types of dopey emails.

When you start looking for businesses to buy or investments, beware of the polished salesman. If it's too good to be true, it probably is. This is a good scam detector. Promises of fast and easy money are the golden hook that attracts people into questionable businesses. Do your research *before* buying into any type of business or opportunity. It's not that hard to research the investment you're looking at to find out if it's legit or a scam.

HANEBISHO (HIGH END TOILET PAPER)

When I was first starting out, I was just trying to understand the market I so badly wanted to invest in. It was easy to fall into one of the free seminar opportunities that pop up all the time. I've sat through a few, and it's always the same high-pressure sales and tagline: "You're going to miss out if you don't sign up *now*."

I once bought into a seminar that was selling a Real Estate Action Kit. This kit they were peddling was going to be my ticket to success. I thought I could benefit from the materials that guaranteed a successful career in real estate. Once I was home, I took the time to dig through what I thought was going to launch me into the exciting world of investing. It turned out to be a large advertisement to buy more material from these snake oil salesmen. The next day, I contacted the company for a refund. Two days later, I received a call from the same company saying they were having a 50% off sale on the seminar materials. The company was selling garbage, basically expensive toilet paper to uneducated investors like myself at the time.

"There are plenty of wolves out there who "prey" you'll trust them with your money."

In the beginning, it's easy to get caught up in promises of fast and easy wealth. That's not how it works. If it was that easy, then everyone would be doing it. Build a solid infrastructure that will help you find a real path to wealth. The path is hidden to most and hard to stay on if you're not prepared for it.

ANOTHER GREAT NON OPPORTUNITY!

A friend called me out of the blue and wanted to see if I was interested in going in with him on a program that helps you buy foreclosed properties at a huge discount. I said I would look into it and let him know. After I received his packet, I spent about ten minutes researching the company. In just a couple of clicks, I noticed that their website had a copyright date from that year. I figured it was just a startup company that put on well-polished seminars to lure you in. I read some of the reviews, and due to the mostly negative feedback and plenty of bad reviews, I decided to pass on the golden non-opportunity. It only took me ten minutes to find out if it was a real opportunity or not. That saved me $1500.00 dollars. Don't be fooled. Do your homework before you buy into any program.

When we first started the business, I received a personal invitation to attend a free seminar. I decided to check it out with a couple of friends. About ten minutes into the seminar, I knew I was wasting my time. The trap was set. They promised extremely high returns with no money and little effort. Red flag!

By the end of the seminar, I had asked three different salesmen how many deals they had done after they went through the courses. None of them would answer me. They pushed me off to other salesmen. I asked them again, when did they go through the program, one salesman said he was getting ready to soon. That did it. I was getting ready to bolt when I noticed my other friend signing up to buy the program. I kept my mouth shut, bit my tongue, and could not wait to see how it played out. The program cost $1,700 for an all-day workshop that was going to teach you how to become a millionaire through real estate investing. Sure!

The next week, when he finished the workshop, actually—I mean when he wasted the whole day getting information that he could have easily found online for free—he said they spent the better part of the day trying to convince him to buy the platinum program which *only* cost $5,000! It sounded like a complete waste of money and time. Thankfully, he did not get hooked into buying the next program.

Polished salesmen who travel from city to city on commission have one goal: to stick their perfectly manicured hands right into your savings account.

Unfortunately, there are plenty of nice, charming people who care about you so much that it would be their pleasure to take your credit card and apply it to hollow promises. Their goal is to see you part with your hard-earned money. These polished salesmen are peddling their neatly packaged garbage that always sounds too good to be true. It's always a good idea to have a skeptical approach at first and then take your time before you make any decisions to buy anything. If you feel any high-pressure tactics—you have to buy this now or else, you won't have the chance to later—**run away**!

Take your time before you decide to part with your money. Research everything.

GUARANTEED 10–25 % RETURNS

In January 2009, a good friend and a couple of his friends were going to a local seminar put on by a real estate mogul named Douglas F. Vaughan. I had heard about this tycoon from the time I was a little kid. I remember his name and face plastered on billboards all over town. He had a great reputation and a growing real estate business.

My buddy was unclear on how Vaughan's investment program worked. It had something to do with real estate holdings being used for collateral—but he was promising 15–25 % returns.

I jokingly said, "It sounds like a Ponzi scam to me." How was anyone able to produce those types of returns in such a down market. I passed on another golden opportunity for a safe, fast, guaranteed high-return investment with one of Albuquerque's greatest tycoons.

HERE WE GO

Two months later, I got a call from one of my attorney clients. They had a summons for us to serve for them ASAP! When I saw the lawsuit, my jaw dropped. I was for Douglas F. Vaughan. The complaint said he had not paid back one of his investors what he had promised, and the investor was suing him. I went to his office, and the receptionist was completely rude and flustered. I could not track the guy down. That night, I found out why. The news broke that Douglas F. Vaughan had pulled off the largest Ponzi scam in New Mexico's history. He defrauded more than six hundred investors for $75 million!

I immediately called my friend to tell him the bad news. He sadly said he gave Vaughan $26,000. Other acquaintances of ours lost at least six figures in his scam. Douglas F. Vaughan was found guilty and was sent to prison for twelve years. If it's too good to be true, it probably is.

Snake oil salesmen will always be spewing their lies and trying to convince people they have all the secrets to fast riches. Buyer beware!

Millionaires are not made overnight; they're made over time.

Can anyone get rich quick? The internet changed the way everyone does business. I'm convinced it is possible to get rich faster if you can find the right niche. I'm sure it's happened for some, but that's not the norm.

If your goal is to get rich quick, you might want to slow down and think about that statement. What's your definition of rich: $100,000, $1,000,000, or $10,000,000? Do you consider quick as one year, five years or ten years? Most of the stories I've heard about people trying to get rich end up usually all the same way: penniless. They don't have the discipline, patience, knowledge, or skills to become true rich.

Remember to take your time and learn how money really works. Money is the most powerful tool in your toolbox. Know the difference between pretend rich (chapter 15) and true rich.

Read and study. Study and read some more. Never stop trying to learn something new. Build up your financial and business intellect. Smart, focused, steady, patient progression takes you to your goals the quickest. You will have a better chance at gaining wealth if you approach it with that attitude.

Try

Investing

Money

Early

CHAPTER 14

TIME

According to Wikipedia, time is a dimension in which events can be ordered from the past through the present into the future, and the measure or durations of events and the intervals between them.

ROADBLOCKS

You want to be wealthy, but you don't spend any time learning the uses of money and how to invest it. However, you have no problem spending 2.2 hours a day on average peeking into other people's lives. You waste one of the most important events that you have complete control over: your time.

Every day, when you wake up, you're given something much more valuable than gold. You're sleeping on top a treasure chest full of 1,440 minutes of this finite thing called time. Your time is worth way more than your money. Once your precious time is spent, it goes into that other category called history. Day in and day out, when time is managed properly, you're writing your own personal history book. It is your own biography. What are you filling your pages with? What great habits are you investing in to help you write your best seller.

When put together with money, your time spent working is one of the main ingredients in funding your investments. Time is the best measure of your progression.

Don't forget that you're the editor. At any moment, you can change what will be written on the next page. You have the ability to write your future with your goals. See where you want to end up—and go make it happen.

> **Time is where this all takes place. Those who have a healthy fear for time will prosper.**

TRY INVESTING MONEY EARLY (TIME)

Try investing your money as early as possible. It's never too late to start, but as time goes on, it gets a little harder. You need time to figure it all out. You need time to make mistakes and plenty of time to recover if mistakes are made. Time seems to be on your side when you're young. One day, you look back and see time for what it really is.

"Don't think you have all the time in the world, just ask anyone over 70."

Life has funny ways of using your time. Sooner or later, it might be marriage, kids, boyfriends or girlfriends, hobbies, sports, or a thousand other areas that slowly eat one unnoticeable minute at a time out of your day. Your days become shorter and shorter due to other time-consuming events. Your calendar gets filled up as your days go on. Time management will need to be one of your greatest strengths.

Time managed correctly will get you to your finish line. Time managed poorly is a trap that will rob you of your focus. Just like driving a car, you need to constantly pay attention to what you're doing to avoid collisions. Pay attention to your time. Respect it—and don't think you have all the time in the world because you don't.

Everyone has the same access to time, but most of us can't even see it. Most of us waste it without even knowing the true value of it. Your time account gets a daily deposit of 86,400 seconds per day, and at the end of each day, your account balance goes back to zero. When you wake up the next day, another 86,400 seconds will be available. If you fail to use these valuable seconds, you will also lose them. No seconds will ever carry over to the following day, and no seconds will ever be saved. This is a set standard for all of us. These rules are fixed and can't be changed; they apply to everyone.

Time does not play favorites, but it rewards those who diligently respect it.

Your life is so incredibly unique. You're living your life second by second, hour by hour, day by day, month by month, and year by year. Own your time, make every moment count, and maintain a healthy respect for your time. Understand how incredibly important time is—and plan to use the time in your account to fully benefit yourself and others.

BEND THE RULES

Philip Stanhope, the fourth Earl of Chesterfield, said, "Know the true value of time: snatch, seize, and enjoy every moment of it. No idleness, no laziness, no procrastination: Never put off until tomorrow what you can do today."

Time's rules are fixed. So, bend the rules to your advantage. Take dominance of your time, own every second of it, and spend it on tasks that constantly move you closer to your goals. Time management needs to be a large part of your plan. It's the same thing when it comes to keeping track of your finances. Keep track of your time. With all the great time-management apps out there, it's worth your time to investigate it.

When your goals start coming together, you'll have plenty of extra resources to hire a housekeeper, a landscaper, a pool-maintenance company, an accountant, and a courier to run all your errands. How much time did you buy yourself in these areas to focus on family, friends, hobbies, and investing?

Bend the rules, and when the time is right, sub out anything that can buy you more time. Purchase time by leveraging other people's skills. Concentrate on the things that will pull you closer to your goals. Time can end up being your best friend—or the opposite.

You get to choose which one you're going to pay attention to. People often forget who the boss is when it comes to their time. Time is a gift, and wasted time is regrettable.

Own it, use it correctly, and prosper.

Hindsight and history will be your trusted gauges to check your progress. Every January find a quiet place to relax and add up your net worth to see if your hitting your financial goals from the previous years. Write down your goals for the upcoming year. This will help you stay on track. You need to see where you've been and where you're going next.

SLOW PROGRESS

If you're not seeing any traction—or it seems to be going too slowly—don't give up. If necessary, try steering your ship in a different direction. All goals and plans must be fine-tuned and adjusted constantly until you see exactly where you're going. Set a course, make plans, and tweak them as you go.

Act now! You don't have as much time as you think you do. Just ask your grandparents how fast time slips away.

As a twenty-year-old, I said, "No way I'm going to be doing this delivery business when I'm forty." I'm forty-seven now. Time is a strange thing. In my mind, I felt like I made that statement yesterday. Twenty years will end up passing you by whether you're investing or doing nothing. Time doesn't wait for anyone.

If you start now, the only regret you will have is that you did not start on your journey earlier.

Time flew by, we managed it the best we could, and I have

absolutely no regrets about how we valued our precious, fleeting time.

GO

You're waiting for what? You'll start when? You can make a thousand excuses before you get started. Do an audit on yourself to see how you can better manage your time. How about get moving now? Do it today! Take a break from any distractions so you can get an idea about what you were put on earth to do. Start laying the foundation for your future. What can you see yourself doing? When you figure it out, go make it happen.

I don't know anyone who became successful by sitting and waiting for something to happen to them. The 1st generation rich know that time is short. Time waits for no one. It moves forward—with or without you. Become a partner with time by using it to your advantage.

You can bend the rules in your favor, but you need to learn how to play the game first. Once you get the hang of the game, everything will get a little easier. Just like everything in life, the unknown is filled with uncertainty and what-ifs. That's what makes this adventure so sweet.

I'M READY

Stepping into the unknown differentiates most entrepreneurs from employees. Some people call it risk-taking, and others look at it as challenges. If you're willing to commit to the path that is not walked on by the masses, then be prepared for change. Good change. You can travel outside your comfort zone and experience something you've always wanted to do. If you want to grab the title of *1st Generation Rich,* start by making your changes today. Don't wait!

Wealth is floating all around us. Build a business that takes part in catching some of that wealth—and then put it back to work in your investments so one day you can sit, relax, and do whatever you want, when you want, and with whom you want. That was our goal, and we reached it. Build something great that changes you and has the potential to change others in the process.

My life could have been a lot different if I had listened to all the negative, unmotivated, pessimistic options from people I thought I respected. Each of those people thought they were doing me a favor by projecting their own ideas on what my limited career path might look like. Those people were talking from their own experiences and fears, which kept them blinded to the real possibilities of other great avenues that can lead to a successful career. I learned very quickly to move away from some and toward those people who did not seem to fit into the mold that was scripted for the masses to follow.

FAKE!

CHAPTER 15

PRETEND RICH

Actors get paid to pretend. The pretend rich pay to act

You never hear about rich people pretending to be poor, but there are plenty of poor people pretending to be rich. Why? They are projecting an image of fake success to their friends and the general public to fool everyone into thinking they are something they are not. Buying counterfeit or phony luxury brands can give the appearance that they can afford the best. They buy high-end brands on credit to give everyone the impression that they are millionaires with stacks of cash stashed in their closets. These are some of the ways the pretend rich try to show everyone they're important and significant.

"There is nothing wrong with pretending... if you are 7!"

The need to project a false image of success and prosperity only leads to stress and a shallow, deceitful existence. Behaviors such as purchasing high-end, brand-name luxury items before they can really afford them will give their friends the impression they are wealthy, but phony props lead to debt, disappointment, and fake friendships.

CHEAP FAKE

In 2002, my wife and I went on a quick vacation to Denver. She saw a little vending cart on the Sixteenth Street mall that was loaded with Louis Vuitton purses for $75. After a little debate, she decided to part with her money to buy the fake purse. The next day, the pin that connected the handle fell apart in the hotel room—and the purse was worthless. We tried to get our money back but the vender disappeared.

This practice of being pretend rich is nothing new. It's been going on all over the globe for thousands of years. If I try to look rich, then people will assume I'm successful and treat me with more respect. If I act rich, I'll be rich someday. That way of thinking is total garbage. Pretend rich is just pretending. If you're pretending you're rich—and never really take the time to build true wealth—you might be stuck in a cycle that can be extremely difficult to break. No one ever gets off a moving roller coaster without being injured.

Unless you decide to move and get a fresh start, it could be hard to change your spending habits and appearance. You'll be stuck playing the pretend game until you go broke!

PRETEND RICH PART II

Over the years I would always see a guy running around town with his fancy toys: high-end sports cars, motorcycles, and designer clothes. I did not know the guy, but he was easy to spot. He carried himself like he was one of the Rockefellers. We both happened to be in a restaurant at the same time. I saw a few people approaching him while he was eating. He would kindly say a few words to his fans and then go back to his meal. Of course, my curiosity was sparked. I wondered who the guy was. Was he famous? I did not recognize him, but it seemed like everyone else did.

A couple years later, I joined a nonprofit that met for lunch every other Friday. As I was enjoying my lunch one Friday afternoon, that guy walked in. He was dressed to a T, dripping with jewelry, and sporting a $1,200 pair of sunglasses. It took me about one second to realize it was the rich, famous guy who everyone else seemed to know. He already knew most of the other guys in the room.

MYSTERY MAN IDENTIFIED

As the weeks went on, I got to know him. We started hanging out after the meetings, and he turned out to be a straight-up fun guy to be around. I could see why people gravitated toward him. He owned a few businesses in town.

When we would hang out, the stories would flow about all the vacations he and his family would take and how hard it was to keep up with all the maintenance for his expensive toys. I naturally thought he was superrich because of the way he bragged, but he sure seemed to be living the millionaire life from the outside.

After one of our get-togethers, he started talking about his businesses, and to my surprise, he shared his income. He had a great income, but it was odd that he was complaining about not having a lot of money in his savings account. He did not think it was such a big deal, but he did mention his credit score was hovering around eight hundred. He was very proud of it.

I asked if he was making money with any of his other investments. He turned to me and said, "The only investment I have are my businesses." He never purchased the real estate they operated out of. He had a large income, no money in his savings account, and not one investment outside of his businesses. Every dollar he made went right out of his pockets in the form of payments to keep up the facade of the rock star lifestyle he portrayed and the six-figure luxury car he was driving. All the hundreds of thousands of wasted dollars were spent on creating a pretend rich lifestyle that fooled everyone, himself included.

He ran into a rough patch, and I never saw him much after that. He spent way too much time and money working on his appearance, but he never gave much thought to having his money working for him.

A façade is an outward appearance that is maintained to conceal a less pleasant or creditable reality.

One of the top reasons many people don't want to save anything for the future is that they want to spend their money the instant it's made. Why not? I could die tomorrow. Let's just live for the moment.

Is the moment worth neglecting your future for? One day, your future will be your present. Then what? Do it correctly with focus and purpose, and one day, you can sit back, relax, and retire with a large net worth and plenty of money coming in from all your different investments. You'll never have to worry about money again. Do it wrong—and you'll wish you paid closer attention to your finances.

Life has a funny way of knocking you off your course and reaching right into your bank account if you let it. Life will divide your attention and prevent you from concentrating on building true wealth. It happens to everyone. Stay the course, finish the race strong, and remember that it's a marathon and not a sprint to the finish line. **Get rich steady**!

CHOOSE WISELY

1. **Closets full of outdated, high-end, overpriced fashionable clothing, jewelry, and expensive luxury cars. No investments.**
2. **Income-producing investments that pay you on a monthly basis and will most likely rise in value instead of losing value. Building your net worth so you will have something to look forward to in the future. Giving you tax breaks and great deductions. You decide to master every dollar you made instead of spending it.**

Instant gratification or deferred gratification? You get to pick—so choose wisely. The choice is easy. The first choice takes little to no effort. Hit a few buttons or swipe your credit card. The little buzz will last for a moment or until your next purchase.

Chase an idea instead of chasing a feeling. The second choice takes focused, purposeful effort, but you will have an abundance of extra money to buy whatever you **want**—and not have to worry about how you will pay for it.

Investing is planting a garden. If the gardener cultivates correctly, prepares the soil, waters, fertilizes, weeds, and fights off all the pests, they will have a large, healthy, plentiful crop over time that everyone can enjoy. Imagine all the options you will have when your crop is harvested.

There is always some sort of payoff when you commit to something you believe in. All ideas start in your mind, and when you're ready to turn it into a reality, just transfer that idea to your limbs.

ARE YOU HAPPY?

You set goals, sacrifice, and do whatever it takes to be successful. You're finally living your dream, but are you happy? Do you have a sense of contentment? If not, how do you find happiness? If you were not happy starting this adventure, you won't be any happier when you're successful.

Why do some of the most successful and richest people on this planet have lives that look like an elephant's cage when the zookeeper goes on vacation for a month and forgets to give the only key to his backup. It is a complete mess. Isn't money supposed to bring you happiness? Money takes away financial worries and will make you more comfortable—but not any happier.

Where does self-confidence come from? Some say self-confidence is found within a person. Others say you're born with it. Self-confidence comes when you step out of your comfort zone, take on the unknown, and push yourself further than you have ever been pushed before. A win and a loss can both build your confidence. Confident people don't care what other people think. You should not care what other people think because there probably not thinking about you anyway. Never base your own unique life on other people's opinions. Be kind, honest, reliable, and dependable. When you say you're going to do something, **do it!**

Just like everything you do in life, after a while, you will gain self-confidence. Practice is the main ingredient that makes life better and finding happiness is up to you.

What keeps you glued to your ideas?

PART IV

MOTIVATION

Motivation is the helium in your balloon. At first, it's easy to get excited and all pumped up about something you read, watched, heard or envisioned yourself doing. After a while, your balloon begins to slowly fall back to earth. The helium begins to escape, and your balloon goes right back to where it started.

You constantly need to refill your goals with a fresh dose of helium in order to keep your dreams afloat. You do this by finding out what motivates you and make it a permanent part of your goal setting strategy.

So, what's keeps you going? What vehicle did you pick to help you achieve your goals? What type of fuel are you using to get to the destination? What type of glue did you choose to keep you motivated?

Time, distractions and life will all eat away at your dreams if you let it. It happens one small unnoticeable second at a time. Then you find yourself right back where you started. Another year goes by then 2 years and you softly settle right back into the same situation that made you want to start your journey in the first place. You settle because you never found the right type of motivation to keep you going. You always have such a hard time completing what you started. That is perfectly normal.

Finding your motivation is the prerequisite before you ever consider starting on your journey.

Bind what motivates you to something strong. It needs to keep you glued to your goals when you fall off the train. So, when this happens, you'll be prepared for it. Motivation is fleeting. What motivates you in the beginning usually fades away as time goes on. Find a strong motivator that sticks around and becomes the driving force that all your ideas will launch from.

Find out what drives you

My motivation was to **work for myself** and **provide** for my family. Those 2 ideas became my passion. That was the glue that kept me stuck to my goals.

Then we fell in love with real estate. That passion is what motivated us to pile up cash to purchase our real estate with. Our business was the vehicle and our passion for real estate was the fuel that kept us highly motivated.

> **Find a motivation that will create a burning desire to complete what you started.**

GEOGRAPHIC
LOTTERY WINNER
BORN HERE!

CHAPTER 16

THE LAND OF OPPORTUNITY

"Trying circumstances breed opportunities for those who pay attention."

According to Immigroup, an immigrant mentality is partly the basis of the American dream. As such, it is a key ingredient for success. The American dream is the idea that every American citizen should have an equal opportunity to achieve success and prosperity through hard work, determination, and initiative.

When I started my quest for financial independence—or having more options—I modeled my journey after my best friend's dad. Cool was a 1st generation Italian from Sicily. He came to America with no education and no money, and he only spoke Italian. How was he able to become so successful starting without any money, help or education?

People who grow up in America fall into the system of going to school, getting a degree, and trying to find a good-paying job. When you find a good job, nothing is guaranteed. Immigrants have a completely different perspective about America.

Immigrants truly believe that this is the land of the free, and they take full advantage of it. When an immigrant sees all the opportunities around them, they don't wait for something to happen to them. They go out and make it happen for them. From starting a business to learning how to finance their investments, immigrants jump in headfirst. They have nothing to lose. If they fail, they still live in the land of opportunities. For an immigrant, failure just means they get to try something different.

Cool decided to become an electrician when he first came to this country. He saw it as an opportunity in a stable profession. On one his jobs, he ended up taking a 110-volt of electricity straight through his body. He took that as a big sign that he needed to try something different. So he did the next safe thing he could think of and became a plumber.

When some doors close, other doors will open. Immigrants see all the vast opportunities in America. They are willing to sacrifice a lot more than the native population to make it. While many people have become complacent, immigrants see America for exactly what it is: a great country with millions of endless opportunities to make their dreams a reality.

Will failure stop your drive to succeed? Will you use disappointment as a crutch and give up? Immigrants come here knowing they have nothing to lose. Most have nothing to gain where they came from. The sad thing is some of the people who already live here have no idea what they could gain. Once all their basic needs are met, it's easy to become complacent and accept mediocrity as greatness.

JOB NON-SECURITY

Sears slashed fifty thousand jobs. The hundred-year-old company closed down hundreds of stores and laid off tens of thousands of hardworking employees. During the Great Recession of 2007–2010, 8.7 million people lost their secure jobs.

Enron filed for bankruptcy in 2001, and 4,500 employees lost their jobs—and most or all of their retirement funds. A lot of them had not diversified. They had every dollar in Enron stock, which ultimately became worthless. People went from being millionaires to just living on social insecurity overnight.

Depend on yourself.

The 1st generation rich work to be in control of their own futures. They invent the games and make the rules. They adjust to changing or turbulent markets and diversify into a variety of asset classes as a safety net so they will always have many income streams working for them all the time. Most millionaires have between three and ten types of income coming from all sorts of asset classes. If one fails, it is okay because they have many backups to pick up the slack. Spread out your risk between different types of investments. Protect your income by adding more income streams to your investments.

I HAVE A RETIREMENT PLAN

Urban Dictionary defines Social Security as a "pyramid scheme run by the US government. They promised to take your money to invest it for you, so you'd have enough to retire on, but from the very beginning, they've just paid the people who are over sixty-five by the money sent in from the workers under sixty-five. For any other organization, doing this would be illegal. They only 'invest' in other government agencies, which means they'll end up being paid back with yet more tax money taken by force from hardworking Americans."

> **The pride that will come from being able to build your own retirement is priceless.**

Let us take care of you. No thanks! I've got this. That should be your answer.

Don't try to depend on the government or someone else who is only looking out for their own interests. The goal is for you to be in control.

When you own the ship, you're the captain. Work like your financial life depends on it. Make the best decisions with the best knowledge possible to steer your ship in the direction of prosperity. Once you have obtained that, your freedom will soon follow.

GEOGRAPHICAL LOTTERY

The average income in America in 2017 was $56,516. At that income, you are in the top 0.85% of the richest people in the world. That makes you one of the 61,369,094 richest people on earth by income. According to ReviewZAP.com, the 2018 federal poverty level for a household of four was an annual income of $24,600. However, you're still among the top 52.48% richest American by income. Globally you're among the top 5.26 percent richest people in the world. You are earning 1,490.91% more income than the global average.

Congratulations, you just hit the geographical lottery, and it's all because of where you were born: The United States of America. That alone puts you at an advantage. Once you grasp how incredibly fortunate you are, try leveraging your good fortune to take full advantage of all the possibilities and opportunities this land has floating around you.

"Dream. Work. Invest. Repeat."

Wake up! and realize that we have more at our disposal now than long-ago kings ever had. Heating, cooling, transportation, food, health care, and running water are at our fingertips twenty-four hours a day and seven days a week. When was the last time you did not eat for a couple of days? Has that ever happened? Probably not. If you work, you will eat, and if you work smart, money will never be distant.

Something out there has your name on it. Find out what it is and become part of this unique class of people who stepped out of their tradition and changed their futures.

THE POVERTY MENTALITY

The poverty mentality is a broken, unhealthy, poisonous way of looking at the world. The poverty mentality will keep you stuck right where you are until the day you die with no options, choices, or real freedom.

Does talking about money make you feel slightly uncomfortable? It shouldn't. The way you grew up has a great impact on the way you view your money. Money being talked about in a bad fashion can end up painting a negative mental picture that can take many years to overcome. If families would talk more openly about money—including its traps, its good uses then, they would have a greater chance of passing on something to the next generation. If you grew up in a family where money was tight, the correct usage of money was probably not discussed around the dinner table.

If no one has taken the time to talk about money's uses and the freedom that comes from investing correctly, a poverty mentality can set in. If you think you'll always be poor, the poverty mentality has taken root. When the root starts to grow, your financial thinking will automatically start to shrink.

How does anyone begin to understand the real uses of money? If your family never talked about it, it might not have been that important to them. School only teaches the basics. How can anyone learn about this great tool if it's not taught properly?

It begins with coming to a place where you are done with the same old ways of thinking.

Do you want to start something new? Do you want a completely new way of thinking? Your outlook needs to be aligned with your actions. The combination of these two simple ideas can change your mind-set.

The poverty mentality can take root when you compare yourself to other people. Why do they have that, and I only have this? A little voice pops up in your head and says, "They must have stepped on someone to get it." The rich keep getting richer, and the poor keep getting poorer. Financial class warfare has gone on forever: the haves against the have-nots or the 1% against the rest of us. Being jealous or envious of other people's situations leads to an us-against-them attitude.

How do you feel when someone close to you is getting ahead? Are you happy for them? Are you envious? Check yourself when someone you know rolls up in a brand-new car. Are you happy for them or covetous? If you can't stand it when you see others excelling and you're not, it's time to change your outlook and align it with a new one.

If you couldn't care less about changing, stop reading now. Don't waste your time. You need to come to a place where you're sick of the same old daily way of thinking and actively train yourself to work toward a new and fresh point of view. Your old way of thinking needs to pass away. Your unhealthy past is no longer going to have any hold or influence on your new healthy future.

If you truly believe in the poverty mentality, you have bought into one of the biggest lies ever told. That lie keeps people from really finding freedom. Think for yourself! Sheep will always follow other sheep. Break away from the pack. Search for successful people who can show you what hard work can produce. The rich will always be there. That will never change. Try using them as an inspiration instead of a crutch.

Familiarity keeps humans comfortable, and when we're comfortable, we tend to lean toward ideas that revolve around security. A sense of security will keep you doing the same thing every day because you know what to expect. The routine that was modeled for you probably shaped how you think about your career and financial decisions.

The influences in your world might be strong, and you might be looking through eyes that were not trained to look for opportunities. You might be looking through the same eyes as your parents and close friends use. You might need to break through the generational thinking that was handed down to you. We copy the actions and mimic those who are closest to us.

Having great influences and positive connections with like-minded people will greatly increase your chances of finding out what makes you great.

The poor mentality is a mind-set that is easy to fall into, but the opposite way of thinking can break it.

THE RICH MENTALITY

A new way of looking at your world through a fresh set of eyes is how you need to approach the rich mentality. Look for opportunities and a chance for a better life. It's about finding a way to get your very own piece of this unlimited pie, which is opportunities and wealth. There will always be deals and businesses that have the potential to make a large profit. Other Investors will never be able to own every great deal out there. You always have a chance to find your niche if you continually look for it.

You can start the rich mentality today! How does it happen? One day at a time. Slow and steady. Think about extinguishing the highly flammable, damaging influences in your life. Work on trying not to be addicted to negative thinking. Toxic and unhealthy behaviors can be a large factor in failure.

The rich surround themselves with positive, like-minded people who need a peaceful non-drama-filled environment to do their best work in. Do whatever it takes to get there. Some changes hurt but change needs to happen in order to give yourself a fighting chance to understand how the rich mentality will completely change your life.

EXCUSES

According to Urban Dictionary, excuses are "tools of incompetence, used to build monuments of nothingness, and those who specialize in them seldom accomplish anything."

Nothing in this life is easy. There is no such thing as get rich quick. If money grew on trees, I would be an arborist. Do not waste your time with fantasies and false realities of winning large amounts of money. Do things right and over time you will become rich. Stick to your plans so your plans have a chance to stick to you. Talk is cheap. Saying something without doing it is weakness. Doing what you say is powerful it can change the world.

> **Be fearless, passionate and excited about your great future.**

NO MORE EXCUSES

I'm too busy. I'm exhausted. I'm overwhelmed. I'm just not feeling it today. Sure, I get it. I've been there. That's how I feel sometimes. It's perfectly normal, but don't use these excuses to put off what needs to be done to reach your goals. Goals take time and energy. There is no such thing as autopilot goals. In the beginning, it's all about executing and developing a strategic plan to help you achieve all your goals. The only excuse for not being able to reach your goals is if you don't make excuses and try making progress instead.

Progress is growth, development, or continuous improvement. Excuses will poison your path to greatness. It's also the perfect alibi for laziness. If you catch yourself making excuses, find out why you're making them, adjust accordingly, and continue back to where you left off. Get back on the train. Find your goals and reread them to energize, motivate, and encourage you. It's easy to forget what inspired you to start this journey in the first place.

I put a few blank sheets in the back of the book. Write down your goals. Once you get your goals written down, transfer them to something you look at all the time. Make them a part of your daily life. Etch, engrave, or tattoo your goals in your mind. Make your goals a permanent part of you. Once your goals are reached, go after new ones. If your goals were a little too big, pare them down a little and begin with smaller goals. Change, reevaluate, and keep on adjusting your specific goals until everyone of them is completed.

IT'S ALL ABOUT YOU.

None of this would have ever happened if I just sat around waiting for something great to happen to us. Do you daydream about having financial successes? Are you hoping that good things will suddenly fall out of the sky or track you down? If that is your thinking, you will probably be waiting an extremely long time.

This is your idea. This is your legacy. You are the driving force behind starting your business and investing.

To act is to take action or do something.

Don't just sit there waiting for something good to come your way. If everything in life was that simple, then everyone would be doing it. So many people miss their opportunities due to inaction.

Change starts in your mind and is executed through your limbs. Do something to make good things happen for you. Make good things come your way. Make good things happen to you.

You're the boss—do what bosses are supposed to do and lead. The faster you learn this, the more time you will have to apply it to every aspect of your life. Change is only an idea. It is only a word. It means nothing until you to make the first move. Change in the right direction will change your life then go and change the world.

HEALTHY FINANCIAL BEHAVIORS + GOALS + TIME = WEALTH

CHAPTER 17

WHAT DO THESE PEOPLE DO?

Healthy financial behaviors + goals + time = wealth.

April and I loved to drive through high-end neighborhoods when were on vacation looking at all the beautiful, homes and fancy cars neatly tucked in their brick-lined driveways. We always asked, "What do these people do? How can anyone afford these massive hilltop dwellings and beachfront fortresses?"

It's practically impossible to know for certain the way these people made their money, but I can say with 100% confidence what they probably didn't do.

AVOID AT ALL COSTS

1. They don't gamble away all their extra money. Instead, they put any extra savings in their investments.
2. They don't get into such extreme credit card debt where they can only pay the minimum balance at 21.28% interest. Never charge anything on your credit card that you can't pay off at the end of the month. This is also how you build a good credit history. Credit will be the number one way to build your wealth down the road.
3. They never use payday loans or cash-advance companies. If you set one foot into one of these fake businesses, you might be a good candidate for financial counseling.
4. They never get in over their head when buying a vehicle. One day, you will have plenty of money to buy whatever type of vehicle your heart desires. Until then, there is no need to pretend you're rich by driving cars that cost as much as a small house.
5. They most likely never had bankruptcies, foreclosures, or repossessed cars.
6. They only buy expensive toys when they can afford them
7. They don't take lavish vacations or eat out at expensive restaurants before they have the money to do so. Use vacations and expensive restaurants as a treat only when your goals are reached.
8. They don't waste time watching TV or spending hours online.

9. The rich pay attention to their credit scores. Having access to capital when you need it is essential for building wealth. They make their time count. They look for investments. They look to build or buy businesses. They work on tax planning with their accountants. They always try to find ways to save money and cut costs.
10. They Fight the urge to impulsively make large purchases before you can truly afford them. Their content with what they have.

"A large investment portfolio is a good indicator of success... not a garage full of toys."

When you don't have money, you want to buy everything—but the opposite happens when you can afford whatever you want. If you want to become 1st generation rich badly enough, you will have to train your impulses to obey you.

If you have all your financial behaviors in check, this list will look like it was written for someone else. If you set out to get rich steady, sooner or later, you'll find yourself living next to the people who own those homes. When you see a fancy home or an expensive car, you're only seeing the by-product of many years of hard work, dedication and reaching goals. It's not really about what these people do; it is more about thinking, *I can do it too!*

THE PERFECT YARD

The landscaping in front of my neighbor's house was a sight of complete perfection with no weeds or trash. All the rocks, plants, bushes, trees, and flowers were perfectly pruned and in an immaculate shape. Even the neighborhood animals seemed to stay far away from his grass. His landscaping was always perfect, but I never saw my neighbor or any type of lawn-care company working on his property.

I caught my neighbor outside one evening, and I had to asked him how he kept his yard in such great shape. He said the secret was getting up right before the sun would rise over the mountains, putting on a pair of gardening gloves, and getting to work. He put in fifteen minutes of work every day. One hour and forty-five minutes per week. I had no idea he had been doing it for years. He was only spending fifteen minutes per day before the hot New Mexico sun would rise, but the outcome was captivating. I never saw any of the work that went into keeping his yard so nice. All I saw was a yard that could have been on the front cover of *Better Homes and Gardens*.

When it comes to lifestyles we admire, sometimes we only get to see the finished products and don't have any real idea what went into it: hard work, sacrifice, planning, saving, and getting up fifteen minutes before everyone else does.

If you have a hiccup in any of these areas, it doesn't mean you'll never be able to find success. Try giving yourself the best opportunities for success that you can possibly have. You can always recover and get back on track, but it's a lot easier if you can avoid all the financial traps when you're starting out. They can knock you off your course and take the wind out of your sails. You will always be able to have the do-over, and the reset button can be pressed easily. I've used the button a few times over the years to recover from mistakes I made, but I continue to push forward and never dwell on my failures.

You're trying to create the most momentum and synergy as possible. When momentum and synergy join your team, things will start happening fast. Getting to that point might feel like it's taking forever, but getting rich steady is a process. A goal-setting, methodical, repetitious marathon will build your investment snowball, and it will naturally start growing on its own. Staying away from financial pitfalls will help you get to the top faster.

BIG SHOVEL

The goal is to generate a high income, but how you do that is completely up to you. We had figure it out on our own since no one went ahead of us and cleared the way. We had to put our puzzle pieces together one piece at time, come up with the goals, and stick with it until our vision became a reality. We constantly reminded ourselves why we began the journey in the first place.

My goal was simple: work for myself and invest in real estate. I found something I had a passion for, and I spent 100% of my time and energy trying to master it.

WHAT IS RICH?

Is it all about being rich—or just having a rich life? Why can't you have both? Or a little bit of each? It doesn't have to be one or the other. A steady balance or a good mixture of each of these will be most satisfying.

We found that true riches come from helping others. I never really had a number in mind when it came to our net worth. I figured if I did the right financial things for long enough, I could end up comfortable—and it worked.

Our happiness never changed along this journey, but our asset column did. Material things may provide comfort—but not a true, lasting happiness. Happiness is found in how you relate to the world around you.

We were always on the lookout and constantly saving, investing, giving and looking for bigger opportunities. We learned the system when it came to financing, taxes, and leveraging, and we used them to our advantage. We mastered our savings and time management; those were critical to conquering each and every goal we set out to achieve.

RICH PEOPLE

My definition of being rich is having the freedom to spend quality time with family and friends on my own terms. If I see a need, I am able to do something about it.

Do rich people have it better than everyone else? Do they have greater access and more privileges than the rest of us? Do most rich people live a high-end, luxurious, pampered lifestyle that we can only dream of? Does being rich equate to having a lot of nice stuff? Does driving high-end vehicles and living in large houses mean you're rich? Everyone has their own idea of what being rich is. What's yours?

TRUE RICHES

A week before Christmas, I took my son to one of our fourplexes with some Christmas presents for some of the tenants. Some of the families at the complex were on some sort of government welfare. Their bare-bones apartments had what they needed and no extras. The kids were all happily running around playing, and the parents had big smiles on their faces. Everyone looked so content.

We talked to one of the tenants as she was cooking, and she said, "Our happiness has nothing to do with money. It is all about having our basic human needs taken care of." She said it was all about the love she had for her family and their friends, which put a smile on her face.

So, is it all about the money? Is it all about being content? Is it a little of both? Is it good friends, healthy relationships, and enough money to put food on the table and pay the bills.

How do you definition true riches?

"The Best Part of Giving is What Happens Next."

PART V

OPTIONS = FREEDOM

Options give everyone freedom.

I want everyone to experience a life full of options. The byproduct of options is freedom. Everyone can have access to both of these.

When I started my journey, I tried talking to as many successful people as possible. I figured they could teach me all the shortcuts to their success. I never really found any useful shortcuts because there is none. Shortcuts are only good if you're driving somewhere. Each person I talked to was able to find a path that seemed to work well for them. Every journey is a customized program tailored to the individuals that are on it.

Go and find something that works with your personality and stick to it. You have an idea; you have the knowledge. Now go plant your seed and make something happen. Go and start something that you were made to do.

Bullseye! Goals Achieved... What's Next?

CHAPTER 18

THE PAYOFF

The best part of giving is what happens next

When I decided to write this book, I had in mind all the people who felt they had no idea what the next step was going to be after high school and those whose lives were not quite going the way they thought they would.

Maybe things have not turned out the way you envisioned them. Maybe you're just in a rut. I was thinking about those people who are not quite satisfied with the path they're on. They are living a boring existence and going through the daily motions to get by. You might feel trapped with no way out. I want this book to inspire you that it is possible to make changes towards a better future. A future that you're in control of. Read and re-read until your light bulb come on.

A job doesn't have to be boring and unfulfilling. Work can be—and should be—exciting. This book was written for someone who always wanted to start, buy, or own their own business or always wanted to give investing in real estate a shot.

I slowly uncovered what the 1st generation rich did to become wealthy, and I set out to mimic their behaviors. Those behaviors turned out to be the greatest factor in their success.

The 1st generation rich are regular, simple folks who never gave up on their goals. They pursued their dreams at all costs to make them a reality. They looked down the corridors of time and saw that they could have whatever they wanted in life by learning and mastering basic financial principles. They ingrained these principles in their minds and repeatedly used them until success started to show up.

1st Generation Rich is an example that anyone can become wealthy over time—and it's never too late to start. Money never discriminates against anyone, but money does favor those who respect it.

I wrote this book to show how it is possible to overcome disabilities by applying simple techniques. I found another way to create a great income and began to build wealth by making my money work for me instead of me trying to work for my money. I encourage and challenge everyone reading this book to follow some of the ideas from our journey to success. Mix these ideas with your own ideas to build a personal plan for accomplishing everything you set out to do.

I engraved certain goals in my mind and took small daily steps toward reaching them. I never lost focus. I learned that frugality was not a cuss word. I still shop at Goodwill once and a while.

I never overspent on anything. When I needed to buy something I would try to get the best possible price. I educated myself by reading and studying successful people in the fields I was interested in.

My best friend's dad had a huge influence on my life. Cool showed me that you don't necessarily need a college degree to become 1st generation rich. That changed everything. Like Cool, we did it with no college degrees, no financial help, no safety nets, and no backup plan if things didn't work out.

We used lots of formulas from this book, but none of them were magic. The magic happened one small step at a time. Getting rich steady was the goal. Taking our time to figure it all out was the plan. We never gave up, and we did exactly what we set out to do. By applying these formulas correctly, we laid a solid foundation for our business and investment portfolio.

By taking control of your behaviors and impulses, you will already be 50% closer to reaching your goals. How far you take it will be completely up to you. It's easy to send out your resume and have a good chance of landing a job. You could end up being stuck at that job while never knowing what it's like to have true options.

> **That's called work jail: being stuck doing something just to pay the bills and never really enjoying what you're doing.**

The entire premise of this book is to bring you to the understanding that you're in control of your life, future, finances, behaviors, choices, actions, career and savings. Those are some of the most important ingredients for building great wealth. Wealth can bring options and freedom into your daily routine.

Never accept mediocrity as being great! Don't let distractions, pessimistic people, or negativity take any type of foothold in your progress. It has a clever, slow way of sneaking into your routine. Guard against all this nonsense. Set out with the goal of changing your situation into an exciting future full of attainable possibilities.

When you look in the rearview mirror of your life, you'll know that you took every opportunity to try to better yourself. You'll never think about what could have been—no regrets, no should-haves, or wish-I-had. You'll have the satisfaction of always knowing that you tried it and gave it your best shot.

We all have setbacks and failures. No one wants to hear that, but it's a reality. Learn from your mistakes, push forward, reboot, keep trying, and find another angle. That's how you get to the finish line.

MY FIRST REAL A+

We were applying for a loan, and the bank did a net worth analysis. We realized all the hard work had paid off when we saw the numbers. All the sacrifice, saving, waiting, and planning showed up on that balance sheet and stared right back at us. It was better than any grade I received in school.

Getting graded by my banker was easy. I spent years building a great credit score and paying close attention to what banks look for when people apply for loans. The best part was when the banker started asking me personal questions about how we built our portfolio.

FROM WALKING TO JOGGING AND THEN RUNNING

This is when the fun begins. Now we're able to capitalize on our hard work. We can build, expand, and see if we can branch out into other new areas. As time goes on, we begin to see things taking shape. Most all our systems have been fine-tuned to produce the cash needed to fund our new ventures.

We started out with a get rich steady attitude. We were slow and steady when we were getting our feet wet. We're moving faster now because we figured out what works and what doesn't work. Our confidence was built by every deal we did. We can step on the throttle and push certain areas we're comfortable with. We can explore ideas we were always interested in. We can take on larger challenges, grow, and expand.

This is the not-so-secret formula to becoming 1st generation rich:

1. **Figure out our goals, passions, and purpose.**
2. **Make your goals a reality. Banish distraction and embrace toil over laziness.**
3. **Build up your new account to only fund your investments.**
4. **Gain the experience and confidence to take on new ventures.**
5. **Build your empire until you want to retire.**
6. **Help others along in their journey to success and purpose.**
7. **Make every day count, live life with determination and no regrets.**

You became an expert in what you do. You were paid well and wisely invested every extra dollar you made. There is no secret to this. Anyone can learn those seven steps. Make the decision to get on the train. Don't be the person who just watches others jumping on board. You get on board and then bring others with you.

"True Rich is when you are able to spend quality time with family and friends on your terms and when you see a need you can do something about it."

OPTIONS ARE FREEDOM

One day I will wake up and ask myself, *Do I* have *to work today—or do I* want *to work today*? When that day comes, I'll know I've achieved my biggest goal: true options combined with endless daily freedom.

WHAT'S NEXT?

Give, give, give. The Italian word for *give* is *dare*. I dare you to be generous with your money. Watch what happens. Generosity benefits both parties.

Every year around Christmas we pick a restaurant with the sole purpose of giving the waiter or waitress a very nice Christmas tip. After we leave the tip, we discreetly leave the restaurant. One Christmas we did this and decided to go back to the restaurant a few weeks later for breakfast. This waitress we came up to us with tears in her eyes saying how much that tip helped her and little daughter that Christmas. Every now and then you get a little glimpse behind the scenes how a little generosity can make a big difference.

The best part of giving is what happens next

A friend of ours takes a vacation to Los Angeles once a year, and he brings a stack of hundred-dollar bills with the sole purpose of giving them out to complete strangers. They said at first, it was a little bit awkward to walk up to random strangers and handing them hundred-dollar bills for no reason at all. After the first few, it started to become addictive. The joy from giving was a rush. Even though a hundred dollars wasn't life changing, it still seemed to give each person some sense of joy and hope. The people who received the money were welling up with tears.

They said it felt so good to give just for giving's sake. Each year, they give more and more. Every year, I can't wait to hear the crazy stories and funny circumstances that happen while they are out giving the Benjamins away.

Give your time, give your money, and give your talents to everyone around you. Once you have the time to invest in other people's lives, try to help them reach their full potential. Give some of your success to others.

ZEAL

I figured there are other people out there who could benefit from my story. Someone might see themselves owning a business with the freedom of being their own boss. Someone might need a little push in the right direction. You can have whatever you work for.

I had to see for myself that the journey was possible—and then I knew there was nothing that could stop me from succeeding.

Becoming an author was never one of my goals. I just figured guys like me with absolutely no experience should be the last person on earth to write a book. I thought books were only written by college-educated professionals.

Then I had this vision. I saw myself walking into the principal's office at Manzano High School with a copy of my book in hand. I wanted to get approval so I could talk to the students that were in the same special ed class I sat in. I figured if I had a book then I would be able to show them exactly how I did it. That vision gave me purpose. My goal was to show that greatness was looking for everyone. I also wanted to prove that once you conceive it, then you can achieve it.

That beautiful vision I had on March 2017 completely changed my life and if I could help someone discover what makes them great then I accomplished my greatest goal to date.

ADRENALINE

Get excited about your future. Don't wait! Start now. Figure it out. Get on the train. Get help if you're stuck.

Dig, read, try, find, and do it! If something doesn't quite work,

try something else. Keep going. Don't give up. Do or die trying is your attitude. Having no safety nets to catch you will keep you focused.

Once you start this journey, you have to finish it. Don't give yourself the option to quit. Follow through until you make it happen. Words like *no, I can't, failure,* and *impossible* should be foreign to you. Work on changing your thinking and then your habits.

Every day, you're writing a history book about yourself. Fill the pages with plenty of great material. By the time you're done writing your story, you will having enough material on how you dreamed, worked, saved, invested, and became 1st generation rich.

FINAL THOUGHTS

Keep in mind that all of this is not supposed to be complicated. The complicated part is saying focused on your habits, saving, ideas and goals until you mastered them. Once you do that then nothing can stop you.

Read, Pursue, Execute, Save, and Repeat

- **Read:** Find books and biographies that inspire you. Listen to business and investing podcasts.
- **Pursue:** Investigate businesses and investments that interest you. Associate with successful people in the areas you're interested in pursuing.
- **Execute:** Take the steps in order to achieve your goals. Be a doer and not just a talker. Move and make it happen. Action is where it's at.
- **Save:** Constantly put away as much money as possible. I suggest becoming sort of a money hoarder. Save, save, save. Pare spending down to the bare minimum. Respect every dollar you make. Do what it takes to build a large investment account. Every dollar brings you that much closer to your goals. Being called frugal is an honor, but don't be cheap.
- **Repeat.**

SEQUENCE OF EVENTS

1. Start by writing down your short-term and long-term goals. This will be the blueprint for building your ideas.
2. Open a new savings named **"Investment Account."** All the money put in will only go toward your investments.
3. Start funding the new account as soon as you can. Every extra dollar you make should end up in this account. The money will be the fuel you put into your investment engine.
4. Once the investment account builds up, start looking for investments to regrow your savings. The larger the savings, the more opportunities you will have to look at.
5. Become an expert in something you're drawn to or are interested in. Sooner or later, you'll have to try something and get your feet wet. Not all passions or opportunities come immediately. Simply start down a path and see where it leads you. If you need to change directions and move down another path, do it. Keep going until you find your fit. The only people who never find their fit are the ones who give up.
6. The endgame is to have all your investments paying you a nice income each month. Build up your investment account in order to buy income-producing assets. The cycle will continue, and your financial snowball will build up.
7. One day, you will wake up asking yourself, "Do I have to go to work today—or do I want to go to work today?" I made this one of my goals. Unfortunately, most people will never have this option. Due to poor planning and unforeseen circumstances, they are stuck just trying to get by. If you take the time to think about your future and do something about it now, you will have a lot less stress down the road.

This journey we started was completely different from what I first imagined. I was looking for one thing and stumbled onto something better. I was digging for gold, but I found red diamonds instead. What we did was no accident. Luck had little to do with our success. We put a plan in motion that provided us with the best blueprints for building our future, and it was the options that gave us the most freedom.

By writing this book, I wanted to show how anyone can do what we did. I have no letters after my name and no diplomas hanging on my walls. I was a dropout from a community college. I am color-blind, special-educated **dreamer** with a touch of dyslexia.

However, I can tell you that anyone can try to start a business. You can invest in something you love and make money doing it. No matter where you are in life, you can use these simple principles to build a great future and your retirement.

I had three strikes against me. I could have used them as a crutch at any time. Instead, I felt like I was in gifted classes instead of special ed. I tried to focus on my strengths and concentrate on them instead of believing the title that was given to me in second grade.

I was inspired by a 1st generation immigrant who showed me that some paths don't necessarily need a college degree. Great ideas and hard work can give you whatever you want in life. Look beyond what every else is doing and find a path that leads to your greatness. Once you arrive help others with their journey.

Go find your own path—the path that fits you.

In the end, it's all about creating more options for yourself. The freedom is worth all the work. That is how we were able to become 1st generation rich. Go find your uniqueness and turn it into something great.

Make sure you have no regrets. The only regret you should have is that you didn't start this journey sooner.

1$T G.R

Make peace with your money?

> **Peace:** freedom form disquieting or oppressive thoughts or emotions.
>
> Marrian Webster

Starting from the day you were born till the day you die money will be involved in every area of your life. Like it or not money effects everything and everyone in some way or another.

Money influences our relationships, careers, health care, longevity and retirement. Because your money is so prevalent and has this much of an impact on everything you touch then why not do whatever it takes to make peace with it. What flows from finding this peace will eventually spill over to every corner of your life.

Know that peace with your money is possible when you make a commitment to diligently searching for it. Making peace within your finances is something that everyone can achieve. The benefits are worth all the work it takes to discover it.

Peace will never knock on your door. It will never try to track you down. Peace is not hiding from you it's usually the other way around.

Once you find peace and it takes hold within your finances watch how everything will change for good. This change is great because it touches everyone and everything around you.

Good things usually happen by purpose, not by accident.

Having Peace with $ = Freedom!

Web site is: markjmigliaccio.com

E- mail is: the1stgenerationrich@gmail.com

Note: The blank sheets in the back of the book are for notes, writing goals, and inspiring quotes.